Earth Science Experiments

EXPERIMENTS FOR FUTURE SCIENTISTS

Earth Science Experiments

Edited by **Aviva Ebner, Ph.D.**

CHELSEA HOUSE
An Infobase Learning Company

EARTH SCIENCE EXPERIMENTS

Chelsea House
An imprint of Infobase Learning
132 West 31st Street
New York NY 10001

Library of Congress Cataloging-in-Publication Data
Earth science experiments/edited by Aviva Ebner.
   p.cm.—(Experiments for future scientists)
Includes index.
ISBN 978-1-60413-854-2
1. Earth sciences—Experiments—Juvenile literature. I. Ebner, Aviva. II. Title. III. Series.
QE29.E2735 2011
550.78—dc22
                         2010043261

Chelsea House books are available at special discounts when purchased in bulk quantities for businesses, associations, institutions, or sales promotions. Please call our Special Sales Department in New York at (212) 967-8800 or (800) 322-8755.

You can find Chelsea House on the World Wide Web at http://www.infobasepublishing.com

All links and Web addresses were checked and verified to be correct at the time of publication. Because of the dynamic nature of the Web, some addresses and links may have changed since publication and may no longer be valid.

Editor: Frank K. Darmstadt
Copy Editor for A Good Thing, Inc.: Milton Horowitz
Project Coordination: Aaron Richman
Art Director: Howard Petlack
Production: Shoshana Feinstein
Illustrations: Hadel Studios
Cover printed by: Yurchak Printing, Landisville, Pa.
Book printed and bound by: Yurchak Printing, Landisville, Pa.
Date printed: June 2011
Printed in the United States of America

10 9 8 7 6 5 4 3 2 1

Contents

Preface

Educational representatives from several states have been meeting to come to an agreement about common content standards. Because of the No Child Left Behind Act, there has been a huge push in each individual state to teach to the standards. Teacher preparation programs have been focusing on lesson plans that are standards-based. Teacher evaluations hinge on evidence of such instruction, and various districts have been discussing merit pay for teachers linked to standardized test scores.

The focus in education has shifted to academic content rather than to the learner. In the race to raise test scores, some schools no longer address all areas of a well-rounded education and have cut elective programs completely. Also, with "high-stakes" standardized testing, schools must demonstrate a constant increase in student achievement to avoid the risk of being taken over by another agency or labeled by it as failing. The appreciation of different talents among students is dwindling; a one-size-fits-all mentality has taken its place. While innovative educators struggle to teach the whole child and recognize that each student has his or her own strengths, teachers are still forced to teach to the test. Perhaps increasing test scores helps close the gap between schools. However, are we creating a generation of students not prepared for the variety of careers available to them? Many students have not had a fine-arts class, let alone been exposed to different fields in science. We *must* start using appropriate strategies for helping all students learn to the best of their abilities. The first step in doing this is igniting a spark of interest in a child.

Experiments for Future Scientists is a six-volume series designed to expose students to various fields of study in grades five to eight (though many of the experiments can be easily adapted to lower elementary or high school level), which are the formative middle school years when students are eager to explore the world around them. Each volume focuses on a different scientific discipline and alludes to possible careers or fields of study related to those disciplines. Each volume contains 20 experiments with a detailed introduction, a step-by-step experiment that can be done in a classroom or at home, thought-provoking questions, and suggested Further Reading sources to stimulate the eager student. Of course, Safety Guidelines are provided, as well as Tips for Teachers who implement the lessons. A Scope and Sequence Chart and lists for Grade Level and Setting help the teacher with alignment to content standards, while the experiments themselves help students and adults think outside the paradigm of typical activities used in most science programs.

Science is best learned by "doing." Hands-on activities and experiments are essential, not only for grasping the concepts but also for generating excitement in today's youth. In a world of video games, benchmark tests, and fewer course choices, the experiments in these books will bring student interest back to learning. The goal is to open a child's eyes to the wonders of science and perhaps imbue some "fun" that will inspire him or her to pursue a future in a field of science. Perhaps this series will inspire some students to become future scientists.

— Aviva Ebner, Ph.D.
Faculty, University of Phoenix Online;
Faculty, Brandman University; and
Educational Consultant/Administrator K-12
Granada Hills, California

Acknowledgments

I thank the following people for their assistance and contributions to this book: Mindy Perris, science education expert, New York City Board of Education District 24, for her suggestions and samples of experiments; Janet Balekian, administrator/science educator of SIAtech schools in Los Angeles, for experiment suggestions; Boris Sinofsky, retired Los Angeles Unified School District science teacher and mentor, for his evaluation of experiments; Dr. Esther Sinofsky, Director of Instructional Media Services for Los Angeles Unified School District, for assisting with research; Michael Miller, educator, and Cassandra Ebner, college student, for their help with the glossary and index; Aaron Richman of A Good Thing, Inc., for his publishing services, along with Milton Horowitz, also of A Good Thing, Inc., for always providing support and a personal touch to any project; and Frank K. Darmstadt, executive editor, Chelsea House, for his consistent hard work and his confidence in me.

This volume is dedicated to the 2007–2008 staff and students of LEAP Academy, which was located in Chatsworth, California. A fine group of individuals became a cohesive community and showed that everyone has the opportunity to succeed.

Introduction

Whether or not students show a spark for pursuing a career in a branch of Earth science, students will require knowledge about the Earth, the Earth's resources, man's impact on the Earth, and how phenomena occur on the Earth and in the surrounding atmosphere. Such knowledge may lead to a deeper appreciation for the Earth's resources and the role people play in maintaining these resources. Earth science also allows students to make connections between what otherwise seem like unrelated areas of science. Earth science encompasses physics, geology, geography, meteorology, mathematics, chemistry, and biology. By integrating knowledge from these scientific disciplines, one can study the Earth's spheres: lithosphere, hydrosphere, atmosphere, and biosphere.

Most students have heard about global warming, climate change, natural disasters, and other events without even realizing that they have learned a little bit about Earth science. But how many students know that atmospheric scientists study the global dynamics of climate; that geochemists study the distribution of major and trace elements across the Earth; that geomorphologists study the Earth's landscapes; that glacial geologists study the movement of glaciers; that meteorologists study the atmosphere and weather; that oceanographers study the physical, chemical, biological, and geological aspects of the ocean; that paleontologists study fossils; or that seismologists study earthquakes? These are just a few of the fields of study in Earth science that could be part of the future of many young boys and girls if they are given the opportunity to explore these topics.

In *Earth Science Experiments*, children will be exposed to various subjects within the discipline of Earth science so that they can explore the Earth from their home or school laboratory and perhaps develop an interest in a future career in a related field. Students can simulate or study weather phenomena in these experiments: "Tornadoes," "Hurricanes," and "Creating Lightning." Others may be drawn to understanding natural disasters in these experiments: "Recording Earthquakes," "Tsunamis," and "Volcanoes." Current topics, as covered in "Global Warming," "Greenhouse Gases," and "Smog," could enhance understanding of current events or local environmental issues. Other students may be interested in studying what lies beyond the Earth's atmosphere in "Solar

System" and "The Moon." Future geologists will enjoy "Geologic Time Scale," "Weathering," "Plate Boundaries," "The Rock Cycle," "Porosity of Rocks," and "Mining." Some students may be curious about "Mirages—Reflections and Refractions at Boundary Layers," while others may show interest in "Building a Hele-Shaw Cell" and "Using a Hele-Shaw Cell."

Each experiment starts with an introduction. Italicized words and expressions therein are listed in the glossary.

So get ready to recreate poor weather conditions, simulate an earthquake, model photochemical smog, go mining for chocolate chips, make your own lightning, and stare up at the night sky. The Earth is a big place, and there is plenty to learn about it.

Safety Guidelines

REVIEW BEFORE STARTING ANY EXPERIMENT

Each experiment includes special safety precautions that are relevant to that particular project. These do not include all the basic safety precautions that are necessary whenever you are working on a scientific experiment. For this reason, it is absolutely necessary that you read and remain mindful of the General Safety Precautions that follow. Experimental science can be dangerous and good laboratory procedure always includes following basic safety rules. Things can happen quickly while you are performing an experiment—for example, materials can spill, break, or even catch on fire. There will not be time after the fact to protect yourself. Always prepare for unexpected dangers by following the basic safety guidelines during the entire experiment, whether or not something seems dangerous to you at a given moment.

We have been quite sparing in prescribing safety precautions for the individual experiments. For one reason, we want you to take very seriously the safety precautions that are printed in this book. If you see it written here, you can be sure that it is here because it is absolutely critical.

Read the safety precautions here and at the beginning of each experiment before performing each lab activity. It is difficult to remember a long set of general rules. By rereading these general precautions every time you set up an experiment, you will be reminding yourself that lab safety is critically important. In addition, use your good judgment and pay close attention when performing potentially dangerous procedures. Just because the book does not say "Be careful with hot liquids" or "Don't cut yourself with a knife" does not mean that you can be careless when boiling water or using a knife to punch holes in plastic bottles. Notes in the text are special precautions to which you must pay special attention.

GENERAL SAFETY PRECAUTIONS

Accidents can be caused by carelessness, haste, or insufficient knowledge. By practicing safety procedures and being alert while conducting experiments, you can avoid taking an unnecessary risk. Be sure to check the individual experiments in this book for additional safety regulations and adult supervision requirements. If you will be working in a laboratory, do not work alone. When you are working off site, keep in groups with a minimum of three students per group, and follow school rules and state legal requirements for the number of supervisors required. Ask an adult supervisor with basic training in first aid to carry a small first-aid kit. Make sure everyone knows where this person will be during the experiment.

PREPARING

- Clear all surfaces before beginning experiments.
- Read the entire experiment before you start.
- Know the hazards of the experiments and anticipate dangers.

PROTECTING YOURSELF

- Follow the directions step by step.
- Perform only one experiment at a time.
- Locate exits, fire blanket and extinguisher, master gas and electricity shut-offs, eyewash, and first-aid kit.
- Make sure there is adequate ventilation.
- Do not participate in horseplay.
- Do not wear open-toed shoes.
- Keep floor and workspace neat, clean, and dry.
- Clean up spills immediately.
- If glassware breaks, do not clean it up by yourself; ask for teacher assistance.
- Tie back long hair.
- Never eat, drink, or smoke in the laboratory or workspace.
- Do not eat or drink any substances tested unless expressly permitted to do so by a knowledgeable adult.

USING EQUIPMENT WITH CARE

- Set up apparatus far from the edge of the desk.
- Use knives or other sharp, pointed instruments with care.

- Pull plugs, not cords, when removing electrical plugs.
- Clean glassware before and after use.
- Check glassware for scratches, cracks, and sharp edges.
- Let your teacher know about broken glassware immediately.
- Do not use reflected sunlight to illuminate your microscope.
- Do not touch metal conductors.
- Take care when working with any form of electricity.
- Use alcohol-filled thermometers, not mercury-filled thermometers.

USING CHEMICALS

- Never taste or inhale chemicals.
- Label all bottles and apparatus containing chemicals.
- Read labels carefully.
- Avoid chemical contact with skin and eyes (wear safety glasses or goggles, lab apron, and gloves).
- Do not touch chemical solutions.
- Wash hands before and after using solutions.
- Wipe up spills thoroughly.

HEATING SUBSTANCES

- Wear safety glasses or goggles, apron, and gloves when heating materials.
- Keep your face away from test tubes and beakers.
- When heating substances in a test tube, avoid pointing the top of the test tube toward other people.
- Use test tubes, beakers, and other glassware made of Pyrex™ glass.
- Never leave apparatus unattended.
- Use safety tongs and heat-resistant gloves.
- If your laboratory does not have heatproof workbenches, put your Bunsen burner on a heatproof mat before lighting it.
- Take care when lighting your Bunsen burner; light it with the airhole closed and use a Bunsen burner lighter rather than wooden matches.

- Turn off hot plates, Bunsen burners, and gas when you are done.
- Keep flammable substances away from flames and other sources of heat.
- Have a fire extinguisher on hand.

FINISHING UP

- Thoroughly clean your work area and any glassware used.
- Wash your hands.
- Be careful not to return chemicals or contaminated reagents to the wrong containers.
- Do not dispose of materials in the sink unless instructed to do so.
- Clean up all residues and put in proper containers for disposal.
- Dispose of all chemicals according to all local, state, and federal laws.

BE SAFETY CONSCIOUS AT ALL TIMES!

1. TORNADOES

Introduction

Every year, there are about 800 *tornadoes* in the United States. Tornadoes are violent, rotating columns of air that are in contact with both the ground and a thunderstorm cloud. In the United States, tornadoes most frequently occur east of the Rockies and cause devastating damage. Thunderstorms in "Tornado Alley," as parts of the United States prone to tornadoes are called, often form near dry areas even though thunderstorms are made of moist, wet air. This combination can create favorable conditions for a *funnel cloud*. When winds at different *altitudes* blow at different speeds, *wind shear* occurs and can create a rotating column of air. If that air is sucked into an *updraft*, the air speed increases, causing a funnel cloud. When the funnel cloud touches down on the ground, it is called a tornado. The strength of a tornado is rated on the *Fujita scale* by how much damage it causes.

In this activity, you will simulate a tornado and observe the effects.

Time Needed

45 minutes

What You Need

- wood, 10 in. x 12 in. (about 25 cm x 30 cm)
- glue gun
- gloves, rubber or latex
- small ceramic cup or dish

✎ small, handheld fan

✎ clear-plastic plant saucer or clear-plastic dish, about 7 in. (18 cm) across

✎ scissors

✎ water, 1/2 cup (120 ml)

✎ dry ice, a few, small pieces

✎ 2 vinyl sheets, about 9 in. x 10 in. (23 cm x 25 cm)

Safety Precautions

Please review and follow the safety guidelines at the beginning of this volume. Be sure to wear gloves as directed.

What You Do

1. Glue the ceramic dish to the center of the piece of wood (Figure 1).

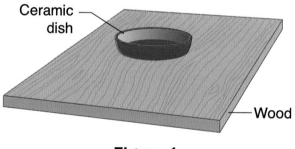

Ceramic dish

Wood

Figure 1

2. Position 1 vinyl sheet so that the longer side is touching the wood, and glue the edge to the ceramic dish (Figure 2).

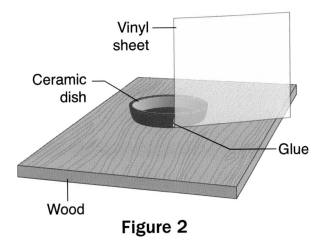

Figure 2

3. Curve the vinyl sheet around the dish without touching it, and glue the vinyl where it meets the wood so it remains in a semi-circle (Figure 3).

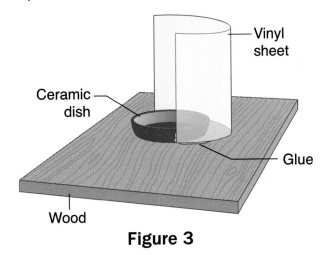

Figure 3

4. Repeat steps 2 and 3 with the second piece of vinyl, but glue it to the opposite side of the dish (Figure 4).

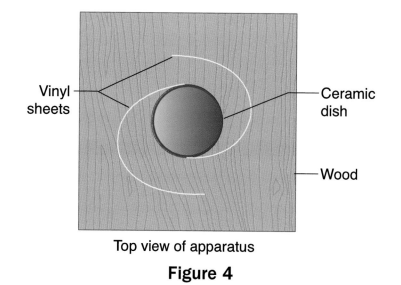

Top view of apparatus

Figure 4

5. Cut a 2-in. (5-cm) hole into the bottom of the clear-plastic dish (Figure 5).

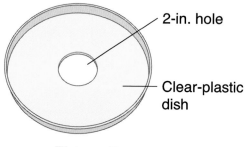

Figure 5

6. Set aside the clear-plastic dish where you can readily reach it.
7. Pour 1/2 cup (120 ml) water into the ceramic dish.
8. Put on the gloves so that you can handle the dry ice safely.
9. Drop the pieces of dry ice into the water in the dish.
10. Turn the clear-plastic dish upside down and rest it on top of the vinyl sheets (Figure 6).

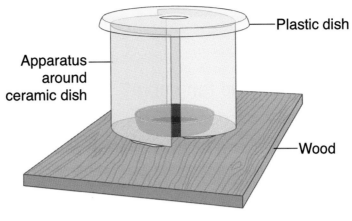

Plastic dish

Apparatus
around
ceramic dish

Wood

Figure 6

11. Set the fan face-up over the hole in the clear-plastic dish and turn the fan on (Figure 7).

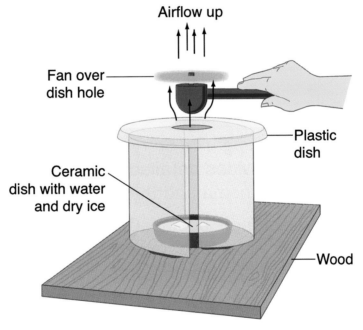

Airflow up

Fan over
dish hole

Plastic
dish

Ceramic
dish with water
and dry ice

Wood

Figure 7

12. Observe what happens.

 **Observations**

1. What purpose did the fan serve?
2. Why was the dry ice needed?
3. What is the difference between a funnel cloud and a tornado?
4. How does a real tornado occur?

Our Findings

Please refer to the Our Findings appendix at the back of this volume.

Further Reading

Challoner, Jack. *Hurricane and Tornado*. New York: DK Children, 2004. Illustrated children's reference book with photographs of actual tornadoes.

Mathis, Nancy. *Storm Warning: The Story of a Killer Tornado*. Austin, TX: Touchstone, 2008. Provides detailed information about the tornadoes of 1999 in Oklahoma and the victims of the tornadoes.

"Tornado." *The Columbia Encyclopedia*, 6th ed. 2008. Available online. URL: http://www.encyclopedia.com/doc/1E1-tornado.html. Accessed April 9, 2010. Encyclopedia entry defining tornadoes and explaining the Fujita scale for measuring their strength.

"Tornadoes." Federal Emergency Management Agency, 2010. Available online. URL: http://www.fema.gov/kids/tornado.htm. Accessed April 9, 2010. FEMA's Web site for children provides advice for children on what to do in the case of a tornado.

———. National Oceanic and Atmospheric Administration, 2010. Available online. URL: http://www.nssl.noaa.gov/edu/safety/ tornadoguide.html. Accessed April 9, 2010. Official government Web site regarding national weather provides a succinct explanation of the causes of tornadoes.

2. RECORDING EARTHQUAKES

Introduction

Earthquakes occur when there is sudden movement along breaks in the Earth's *crust*. The *hypocenter*, or *focus*, of an earthquake is the actual location under the Earth's surface where the earthquake occurred. The *epicenter* is the spot on the surface of the Earth above the hypocenter where the earthquake originated. Earthquakes can be recorded with a *seismograph*. The information on the seismograph is interpreted using the *Richter scale* to determine the intensity of an earthquake. The Richter scale is a base-10 logarithmic scale, so each increase by 1 on the scale is actually a difference of 10 times in terms of intensity. For example, a *magnitude* 5.0 earthquake is 10 times stronger than a magnitude 4.0 earthquake.

In this activity, you will simulate the manner in which a seismograph records earthquake activity.

Time Needed

15 minutes

What You Need

- ✎ licensed adult driver
- ✎ automobile
- ✎ pad of paper, legal size preferable
- ✎ fine-point, felt-tip black marker
- ✎ clock or timer

Safety Precautions

Please review and follow the safety guidelines at the beginning of this volume.

What You Do

1. Sit in a passenger seat in the vehicle. The front passenger side is preferable, but if there are age or safety restrictions preventing you from doing so, sit in the back seat. Make sure you wear a seat belt!

2. Hold the pad of paper sideways (Figure 1).

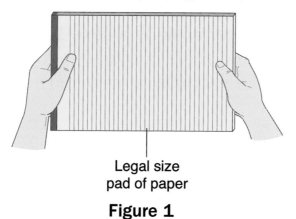

Legal size
pad of paper

Figure 1

3. Keeping the pad of paper sideways, hold the pad in place with one hand against the nearest surface—e.g., glove compartment or seat in front of you (Figure 2).

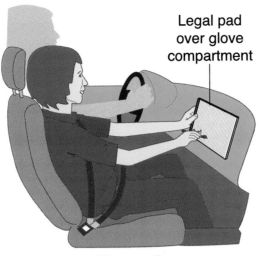

Legal pad
over glove
compartment

Figure 2

4. Remove the cap from the marker and hold it in your other hand.

5. With your arm stretched out, make sure that the tip of the marker can touch the paper (Figure 3).

Legal pad   Marker

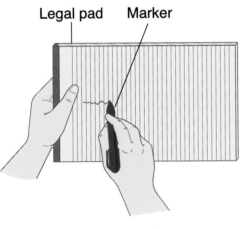

Figure 3

6. Have a licensed adult drive along a bumpy road or highway for about 2 minutes.

7. During the drive, slowly move your hand with the marker from left to right across the paper (this should take about 7 to 10 seconds) without preventing the bumpy ride from moving your hand up and down (Figure 4).

Seismographic-like marks   Marker

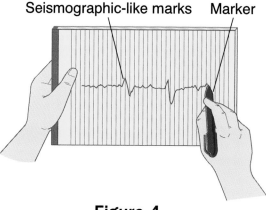

Figure 4

8. Each time you come to the end of the paper, flip the page and repeat steps 7 and 8.

 **Observations**

1. Did your arm move up or down significantly when you hit a bump or pothole in the road?
2. What evidence do you have to show that your arm moved?
3. How does this activity simulate a seismograph?
4. How could you make a scale for your street seismograph that would be like the Richter scale used for earthquakes?

Our Findings

Please refer to the Our Findings appendix at the back of this volume.

Further Reading

"Earthquakes." *USGS.gov*. 2010. Available online. URL: http://earthquake.usgs.gov/earthquakes/. Accessed April 23, 2010. Official government Web site of the U.S. Geological Survey that contains up-to-date reports on earthquake activity, magnitudes of the earthquakes, and locations of the earthquakes.

Hough, Susan. *What We Know (and Don't Know) About Earthquakes*. Princeton, NJ: Princeton University Press, 2004. Reviews the state of earthquake science and what we still have to learn about earthquakes.

"Seismology." *The Columbia Encyclopedia*, 6th ed. 2008. Available online. URL: http://www.encyclopedia.com/doc/1E1-seismolo.html. Accessed April 23, 2010. Shows seismic charts and related tables about earthquakes.

"Welcome." SCEDC. 2010. Available online. URL: http://www.data.scec.org/. Accessed April 23, 2010. Contains links to information about earthquakes specifically in California.

Yanev, Peter, and Andrew Thompson. *Peace of Mind in Earthquake Country: How to Save Your Home, Business, and Life*. San Francisco: Chronicle Books, 2009. Written by a seismic engineer and a risk consultant, the book provides practical solutions to avoiding loss of life and property due to earthquakes.

3. HURRICANES

Introduction

A *hurricane* is defined as a cyclone in which winds reach more than 74 miles per hour. In some instances, hurricane wind speeds have been documented to reach more than 190 miles per hour. The term *hurricane* is usually reserved for those storms with related wind speeds that occur over the North Atlantic Ocean. Equivalent storms in the West Pacific are known as *typhoons*, those in the Indian Ocean as *tropical cyclones*. Hurricanes originate over the ocean as several storms, creating a low-pressure center, while higher in the *atmosphere*, the high pressure creates an outward force. This causes the cyclone to spin, eventually passing through the *tropical depression* stage into the *tropical storm* stage and eventually having winds with such high velocity that it finally becomes a hurricane. The wind intensity is labeled according to the *Saffir-Simpson scale*. A category-1 hurricane causes the least damage; a category-5 is considered catastrophic. Hurricanes occur every year over the Atlantic. The National Weather Service tracks these hurricanes every season, issuing alerts to people living in areas that might be impacted by the storms.

In this activity, you will track hurricane patterns and compare them to patterns from prior hurricane seasons.

 Time Needed
1 hour

What You Need

✎ National Weather Service Web site http://www.nhc.noaa.gov

✎ computer with Internet access

✎ color printer

✎ set of colored pencils

✎ set of colored, fine-point markers

Safety Precautions

Please review and follow the safety guidelines at the beginning of this volume. Follow all Internet safety guidelines when accessing the Internet.

What You Do

1. Visit the National Weather Service Web site and find the maps of prior hurricane seasons.

2. Print out the map of the 2009 Atlantic Hurricane Season. It should be at http://www.nhc.noaa.gov/2009atlan.shtml, but you may need to check the site for updated Web pages.

3. Click on the map to enlarge it (Figure 1).

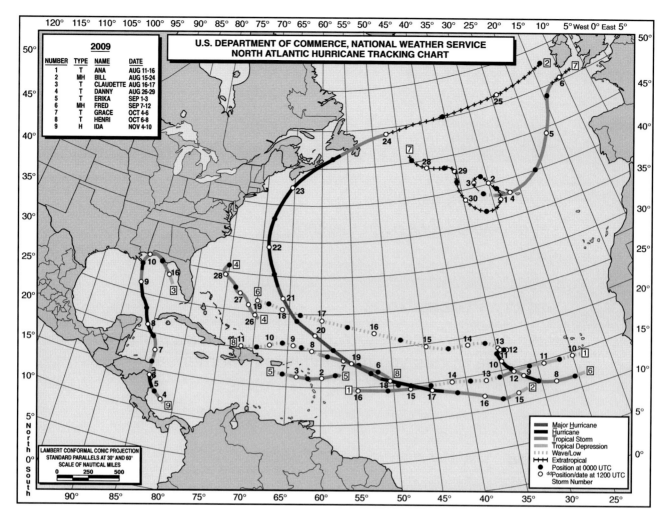

**Figure 1. 2009 Atlantic Hurricane Season, adapted from
http://www.nhc.noaa.gov/2009atlan.shtml**

4. Print the color map.

5. Click on the 2008 Atlantic Hurricane Season. It should be at
    http://www.nhc.noaa.gov/2008atlan.shtml, but you may need
    to check the site for updated Web pages.

6. Using the same colors as in the map key on the 2009 map,
    copy the hurricane/tropical depression tracking information from
    the 2008 map onto the 2009 map (Figure 2).

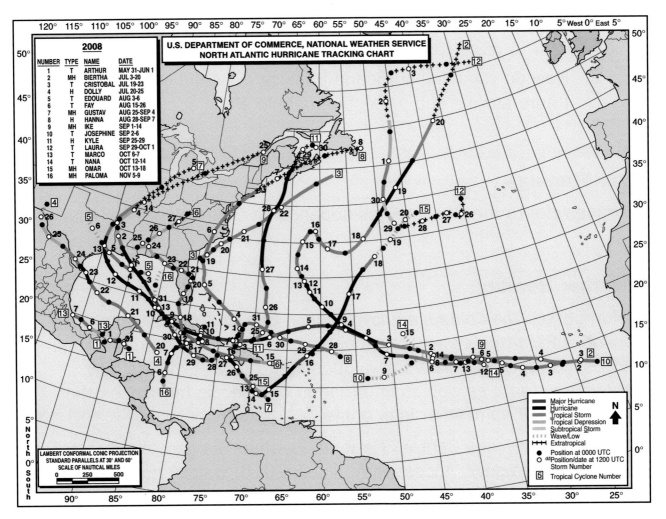

Figure 2. Data from 2008 Atlantic Hurricane Season imposed on map of 2009.

7. Click on the 2007 Atlantic Hurricane Season. It should be at http://www.nhc.noaa.gov/2007atlan.shtml, but you may need to check the site for updated Web pages.

8. Repeat step 6 using the colored markers.

9. Observe your tracking map of three consecutive hurricane seasons.

 Observations

1. Did you notice any patterns in the intensity of the storms from year to year? If so, what?

2. Did you notice any patterns in the location of hurricanes from year to year? If so, what?

3. How do you think hurricane tracking is useful in predicting future storms and protecting people along coastlines?

Our Findings

Please refer to the Our Findings appendix at the back of this volume.

Further Reading

"Hurricane." *The Columbia Encyclopedia*, 6th ed. 2008. Available online. URL: http://www.encyclopedia.com/doc/1E1-hurrican.html. Accessed April 20, 2010. Encyclopedia entry that explains how hurricanes form, as well as information on specific hurricanes that caused major damage or loss of life.

"National Hurricane Center." National Weather Service, 2010. http://www.nhc.noaa.gov/. Accessed April 20, 2010. Official government Web site for weather that also includes historical weather information on hurricanes, as well as how to protect yourself during a hurricane.

"Saffir-Simpson Scale." *The Columbia Encyclopedia*, 6th ed. 2008. http://www.encyclopedia.com/doc/1E1-SafSimpsc.html. Accessed April 20, 2010. Explains the scale for rating the intensity of hurricanes.

Treaster, Joseph. *Hurricane Force: In the Path of America's Deadliest Storms*. Ashmore, IL: Kingfisher, 2007. Written by a journalist for grades 4 through 8, with details about the impact of hurricanes and many color photos and diagrams.

Van Heerden, Ivor, and Mike Bryan. *The Storm: What Went Wrong and Why During Hurricane Katrina*. New York: Penguin, 2007. Very technical and scientific account of how the country was not prepared for one of the most devastating natural disasters in the history of America.

4. TSUNAMIS

Introduction

Tsunamis are large waves that result after an undersea *seismic* occurrence, such as an *earthquake*. However, an undersea volcanic eruption on a large scale can also cause a tsunami. In the United States, Hawaii is at greatest risk for tsunamis, but there have been some in California and Alaska. Tsunamis have occured in other countries, such as Japan, and one of the most devastating tsunamis ever recorded occurred in the Indian Ocean off the Indonesian coast after a large earthquake, killing more than 200,000 people. Today, there are tsunami warning centers around the world to alert people of major undersea seismic activity that might generate a tsunami.

In this activity, you will simulate the conditions that create tsunamis and observe the waves that result.

Time Needed

30 minutes

What You Need

- large spring, such as a Slinky® (Stick figures and springs are not drawn to scale.)
- partner
- tabletop
- large, clear-plastic container, such as a Rubbermaid® storage container
- rubber mallet

enough water to fill the plastic container halfway

✎   unlined white paper, a few sheets

✎   pencil

Safety Precautions

Please review and follow the safety guidelines at the beginning of this volume.

What You Do

1. Sit on the ground and hold tight to one end of the spring.

2. Have your partner hold the opposite end of the spring while sitting on the ground across from you, so that the spring is loosely stretched out in a straight line (Figure 1).

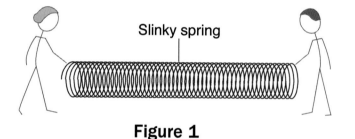

Slinky spring

Figure 1

3. Push on the spring toward your partner without letting go of your end of the spring (Figure 2).

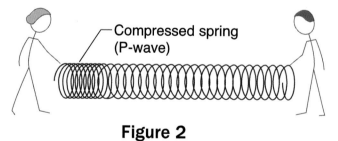

Compressed spring (P-wave)

Figure 2

4. Observe the compression of the spring and the way the wave you created travels. This is a model of a P-wave.

5. Move your end of the spring back and forth along the ground while your partner holds the opposite end steady (Figure 3).

S-wave

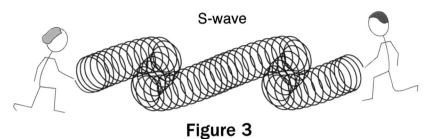

Figure 3

6. Observe the waves you created. This models an S-wave.

7. Lift your end of the spring and snap it, while your partner holds his or her end steady (Figure 4).

L-wave

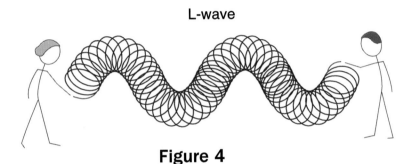

Figure 4

8. Observe the waves you created. This models an L-wave, the type that typically causes tsunamis.

9. Set aside the spring.

10. Fill a large, clear-plastic container with water halfway.

11. Place the container on the tabletop.

12. Hit the front of the table with the rubber mallet (Figure 5) to simulate P-waves.

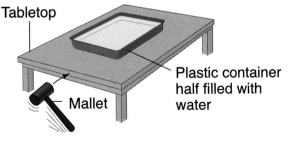

Tabletop

Plastic container
half filled with
water

Mallet

Figure 5

13. Observe the waves created in the water.

14. Draw a sketch of your observation.

15. Strike the side of the table with the mallet (Figure 6) to simulate S-waves.

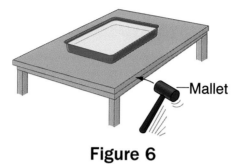

Figure 6

16. Observe the waves this creates in the water.

17. Draw a sketch of your observation.

18. Finally, strike the tabletop in front of the container with the mallet (Figure 7) to simulate L-waves.

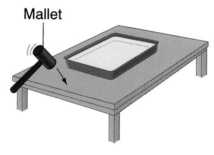

Figure 7

19. Observe the waves this creates in the water. This simulates tsunami waves.

20. Draw a sketch of your observation.

 **Observations**

1. What differences did you notice between the motion of the P-waves, S-waves, and L-waves in the spring?

2. What differences did you notice between the motion of the P-waves, S-waves, and L-waves in the water?

3. How do you think the L-wave motion causes tsunamis as opposed to the other wave motions?

Our Findings

Please refer to the Our Findings appendix at the back of this volume.

Further Reading

Harris, Nancy. *Great Disasters-Tsunamis*. Farmington, MI: Greenhaven Press, 2003. Great book for young adults explaining tsunamis and the devastating damage they cause. This book, however, was written prior to the Indian Ocean tsunami, so it does not include specific information on that tsunami.

Lace, William. *The Indian Ocean Tsunami of 2004*. New York: Chelsea House Publishers, 2008. For ages 9 to 12, recounts the details of the tsunami off the coast of Indonesia in 2004.

National Weather Service. "Pacific Tsunami Warning Center." Available online. URL: http://www.prh.noaa.gov/ptwc/. Accessed April 22, 2010. Official National Weather service Web site for tsunami warnings. Provides up-to-date information.

"The Tsunami Warning System." University of Washington. Available online. URL: http://www.geophys.washington.edu/tsunami/general/warning/warning.html. Accessed April 22, 2010. University of Washington's Earth and Space Sciences' Web site contains information about the tsunami warning system.

Zubair, Lareef. "Scientific Background on the Indian Ocean Earthquake and Tsunami." 2004. Available online. URL: http://iri.columbia.edu/~lareef/tsunami/. Accessed April 22, 2010. Scientific details about the tsunami of 2004, including diagrams, information about warning systems, and background information on the earthquake that caused it.

5. VOLCANOES

Introduction

Volcanoes are ruptures in the Earth's *crust* that allow *magma* to escape from below the surface. Magma is *molten* rock; the extreme temperatures under the Earth's crust keep the rock in a molten state rather than a solidified one. Magma temperatures range from 1,300 to 2,400°F [(degrees Fahrenheit); 700 to 1,300°C (degrees Celsius)]. Once magma leaves a volcano, it is called *lava*. However, before it ever reaches the surface, magma travels through the volcano, forming *dikes*. A dike is what is known as a *sheet intrusion* or magma moving through a vertical sheet-like *fissure* in the volcano.

In this activity, you will simulate how magma moves inside a volcano and how volcanic dikes are formed.

Time Needed

3 1/2 hours to prepare
60 minutes to complete

What You Need

- 4 packets of unflavored gelatin
- mixing spoon
- 3-quart (3-liter [L]) or larger-size bowl
- 2-quart-size bowl (2-L)
- plastic syringe (such as the type found in pet stores for feeding birds)
- bottle of red food coloring

- measuring cup
- clear-plastic cup
- cool water, enough to fill cup about 2/3 full and enough for another 2 cups (473 ml)
- boiling water, to fill 6 cups (1,419 ml)
- timer or watch
- ruler
- Peg-Board,™ about 16 in. x 24 in. (40 cm x 60 cm) with 0.2-in. (5-mm) diameter holes each about 1 in. (2.5 cm) apart. (If you cannot find a Peg-Board,™ you can use a disposable aluminum pan and poke holes in it using a ruler to measure)
- refrigerator
- 4 bricks
- 2 sheets of plain, white paper
- black pencil
- red pencil
- knife

Safety Precautions

Please review and follow the safety guidelines at the beginning of this volume. Adult supervision is recommended when preparing and handling boiling water. Exercise caution to avoid scalding or burns. Adult supervision is also recommended when handling sharp objects like knives.

What You Do

1. Pour the contents of the 4 packets of gelatin into the larger bowl.
2. Add 2 cups of cool water.
3. Stir the water and gelatin for about 30 seconds.

4. Add 6 cups of boiling water.

5. Stir until the gelatin is completely dissolved.

6. Carefully pour the gelatin mixture into the 2-liter bowl.

7. Put the 2-liter bowl in the refrigerator.

8. Allow at least 3 hours for the gelatin to set.

9. Remove the bowl from the refrigerator.

10. Set the Peg-Board™ on 4 bricks, which should be standing lengthwise to raise the Peg-Board™ (Figure 1).

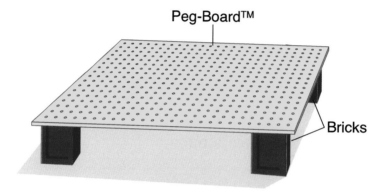

Figure 1

11. Quickly flip the bowl upside down on the Peg-Board™ (Figure 2). The gelatin is a transparent representation of a volcano.

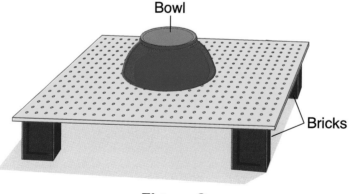

Figure 2

12. Remove the bowl from the gelatin, leaving the gelatin on the Peg-Board™ (Figure 3).

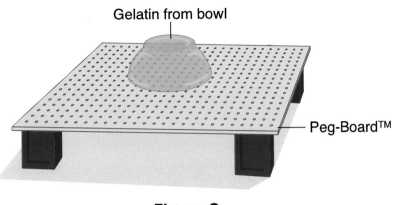

Figure 3

13. Fill a cup 2/3 full with cool water.

14. Add red food coloring until the water is noticeably a red color. The red water will simulate magma.

15. Fill the syringe from the cup of red water (Figure 4). If you see bubbles in the syringe, push out a little of the water from the syringe to remove the bubbles.

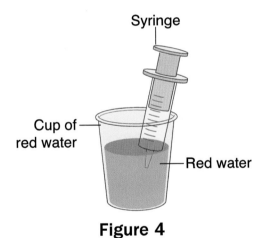

Figure 4

16. Reaching underneath the Peg-Board,™ insert the syringe through a hole in the peg board as close to the center of the gelatin as possible (Figure 5).

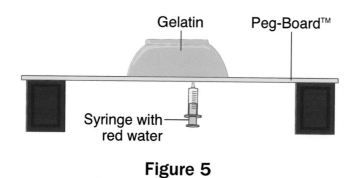

Gelatin   Peg-Board™

Syringe with
red water

Figure 5

17. Slowly inject the red water from the syringe into the gelatin.

18. Observe what happens to the red water and the gelatin.

19. Repeat steps 15 to 18 three more times, except insert the syringe into different holes under different parts of the gelatin other than the center.

20. Looking down on the gelatin from above, sketch on a sheet of paper what you observe in terms of the "magma" and label it "Map View."

21. Cut your gelatin mold in half (Figure 6).

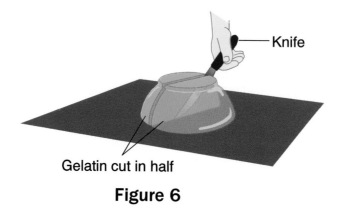

Knife

Gelatin cut in half

Figure 6

22. Observe one of the cut faces and sketch what you see (Figure 7). Label this "cross-section view."

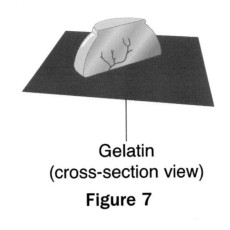

Gelatin
(cross-section view)

Figure 7

 **Observations**

1. How do the gelatin and red-colored water simulate magma moving through a volcano?

2. What did you notice about how the red water traveled through the gelatin when you injected it?

3. Compare the map view with the cross-section view that you drew. Do you notice any differences that you would not have seen if you had drawn only one view? If so, what were they?

Our Findings

Please refer to the Our Findings appendix at the back of this volume.

Further Reading

"Alaska Volcano Observatory." Alaska Volcano Observatory, 2010. Available online. URL: http://www.avo.alaska.edu/. Accessed April 26, 2010. Information about active volcanoes in Alaska.

Grace, Catherine O'Neill. *Forces of Nature: The Awesome Power of Volcanoes, Earthquakes, and Tornadoes*. Washington, DC: National Geographic Books, 2004. For grades 4 through 8, contains scientific facts and impressive photographs and illustrations.

Nardo, Don. *Volcanoes (Extreme Threats)*. Greensboro, NC: Morgan Reynolds Publishing, 2009. Updated book with information about volcanoes and pictures geared toward grades 4 to 8.

"Volcano Hazards Program." USGS, 2010. Available online. URL: http://volcanoes.usgs.gov/. Accessed April 26, 2010. Official government Web site that provides updated information on volcano eruption alerts.

"Volcano World." Oregon State University, 2010. Available online. URL: http://volcano.oregonstate.edu/. Accessed April 26, 2010. Web site from Oregon State University with updated links and articles about modern volcanoes.

6. GLOBAL WARMING

Introduction

Global warming, also known as *climate change*, is caused mainly by the rising levels of *atmospheric carbon dioxide*. Although some carbon dioxide is always present in the *atmosphere*, most scientists believe that the burning of *fossil fuels* creates increased levels of carbon dioxide *emissions*. Since carbon dioxide is a *greenhouse gas*, the increased levels have resulted in slight but persistent increases in temperature. Rising temperatures worldwide are believed to be causing the melting of *glaciers*. In turn, this impacts wildlife and plant life. Additionally, further changes to climate can occur, such as more intense storms, flooding, and even *drought* in some areas.

In this activity, you will prepare a graph of carbon dioxide emissions over a 20-year period and determine for yourself if greenhouse gas emissions have risen over the past 2 decades, impacting climate across the globe.

Time Needed

30 minutes

What You Need

- graph paper
- pencil

Safety Precautions

Please review and follow the safety guidelines at the beginning of this volume.

What You Do

1. Set up your graph (Figure 1) so that the year is on the Y-axis, starting with 1990, and the amount of carbon dioxide is on the X-axis.

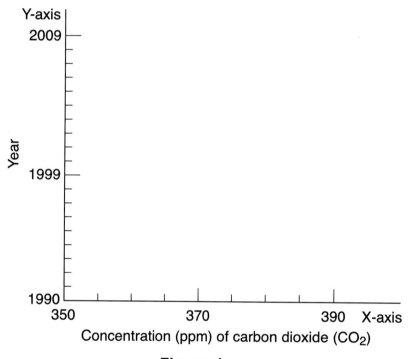

Figure 1

2. Select May as the month of the year for which you will be selecting data (that is, you will use the data for each May for 20 years of data).

3. Using the data table, start with May 1990 and graph the data point for the atmospheric carbon dioxide levels for that year.

4. Repeat step 2 for each year after May 1990 through 2009.

5. Connect your data points.

Data Table. Atmospheric CO_2 Mauna Loa Observatory (Scripps / NOAA / ESRL), Monthly & Annual Mean CO_2 Concentrations (ppm), March 1958-Present*

Year	Jan	Feb	Mar	Apr	May	Jun	Jul	Aug	Sep	Oct	Nov	Dec	Annual
1958			315.71	317.45	317.5	317.11	315.86	314.93	313.20	312.61	313.33	314.67	
1959	315.62	316.38	316.71	317.72	318.29	318.16	316.55	314.8	313.84	313.26	314.80	315.59	315.98
1960	316.43	316.97	317.58	319.02	320.02	319.59	318.18	315.91	314.16	313.83	315.00	316.19	316.91
1961	316.93	317.70	318.54	319.48	320.58	319.77	318.58	316.79	314.80	315.38	316.10	317.01	317.64
1962	317.94	318.55	319.68	320.63	321.01	320.55	319.58	317.40	316.26	315.42	316.69	317.70	318.45
1963	318.74	319.08	319.86	321.39	322.24	321.47	319.74	317.77	316.21	315.99	317.12	318.31	318.99
1964	319.57	320.11	320.76	321.79	322.24	321.89	320.44	318.70	316.70	316.79	317.79	318.71	319.62
1965	319.44	320.44	320.89	322.13	322.16	321.87	321.39	318.80	317.81	317.30	318.87	319.42	320.04
1966	320.62	321.59	322.39	323.87	324.01	323.75	322.40	320.37	318.64	318.10	319.78	321.08	321.38
1967	322.06	322.50	323.04	324.42	325.00	324.09	322.55	320.92	319.31	319.31	320.72	321.96	322.16
1968	322.57	323.15	323.89	325.02	325.57	325.36	324.14	322.03	320.41	320.25	321.31	322.84	323.04

(continued)

Year	Jan	Feb	Mar	Apr	May	Jun	Jul	Aug	Sep	Oct	Nov	Dec	Annual
1969	324.00	324.42	325.64	326.66	327.34	326.76	325.88	323.67	322.38	321.78	322.85	324.12	324.62
1970	325.03	325.99	326.87	328.14	328.07	327.66	326.35	324.69	323.10	323.16	323.98	325.13	325.68
1971	326.17	326.68	327.18	327.78	328.92	328.57	327.34	325.46	323.36	323.56	324.80	326.01	326.32
1972	326.77	327.63	327.75	329.72	330.07	329.09	328.05	326.32	324.93	325.06	326.50	327.55	327.45
1973	328.55	329.56	330.30	331.50	332.48	332.07	330.87	329.31	327.51	327.18	328.16	328.64	329.68
1974	329.35	330.71	331.48	332.65	333.15	332.13	330.99	329.17	327.41	327.21	328.34	329.50	330.17
1975	330.68	331.41	331.85	333.29	333.91	333.40	331.74	329.88	328.57	328.35	329.33	330.55	331.08
1976	331.66	332.75	333.46	334.78	334.79	334.05	332.95	330.64	328.96	328.77	330.18	331.65	332.05
1977	332.69	333.23	334.97	336.03	336.82	336.10	334.79	332.53	331.19	331.21	332.35	333.47	333.78
1978	335.09	335.26	336.61	337.77	338.00	337.98	336.48	334.37	332.33	332.40	333.76	334.83	335.41
1979	336.21	336.64	338.13	338.96	339.02	339.20	337.60	335.56	333.93	334.12	335.26	336.78	336.78
1980	337.80	338.28	340.04	340.86	341.47	341.26	339.34	337.45	336.10	336.05	337.21	338.29	338.68

(continued)

Year	Jan	Feb	Mar	Apr	May	Jun	Jul	Aug	Sep	Oct	Nov	Dec	Annual
1981	339.36	340.51	341.57	342.56	343.01	342.52	340.71	338.51	336.96	337.13	338.58	339.91	340.11
1982	340.92	341.69	342.87	343.83	344.30	343.42	341.85	339.82	337.98	338.09	339.24	340.67	341.22
1983	341.42	342.67	343.45	345.08	345.75	345.32	343.93	342.08	340.00	340.12	341.35	342.89	342.84
1984	343.87	344.59	345.29	346.58	347.36	346.80	345.37	343.06	341.24	341.54	342.90	344.36	344.41
1985	345.08	345.89	347.49	348.02	348.75	348.19	346.49	344.70	343.04	342.92	344.22	345.61	345.87
1986	346.42	346.95	347.88	349.57	350.35	349.70	347.78	345.89	344.88	344.34	345.67	346.89	347.19
1987	348.20	348.55	349.56	351.12	351.84	351.45	349.77	347.62	346.37	346.48	347.80	349.03	348.98
1988	350.23	351.58	352.22	353.53	354.14	353.64	352.53	350.42	348.84	348.94	349.99	351.29	351.45
1989	352.72	353.10	353.64	355.43	355.70	355.11	353.79	351.42	349.83	350.10	351.26	352.66	352.90
1990	353.63	354.72	355.49	356.10	357.08	356.11	354.67	352.67	351.05	351.36	352.81	354.21	354.16
1991	354.87	355.67	357.00	358.40	359.00	357.99	355.96	353.78	352.20	352.22	353.70	354.98	355.48
1992	356.08	356.84	357.73	358.91	359.45	359.19	356.72	354.77	352.80	353.21	354.15	355.39	356.27

(continued)

Year	Jan	Feb	Mar	Apr	May	Jun	Jul	Aug	Sep	Oct	Nov	Dec	Annual
1993	356.76	357.17	358.26	359.17	360.07	359.41	357.36	355.29	353.96	354.03	355.27	356.70	356.95
1994	358.05	358.80	359.67	361.13	361.48	360.60	359.20	357.23	355.42	355.89	357.41	358.74	358.64
1995	359.73	360.61	361.60	363.05	363.62	363.03	361.55	358.94	357.93	357.80	359.22	360.42	360.62
1996	361.83	362.94	363.91	364.28	364.93	364.70	363.31	361.15	359.41	359.34	360.62	361.96	362.36
1997	362.81	363.87	364.25	366.02	366.47	365.36	364.10	361.89	360.05	360.49	362.21	364.12	363.47
1998	365.00	365.82	366.95	368.42	369.33	368.78	367.59	365.81	363.83	364.18	365.36	366.87	366.50
1999	367.97	368.83	369.46	370.77	370.66	370.10	369.10	366.70	364.61	365.17	366.51	367.85	368.14
2000	369.07	369.32	370.38	371.63	371.32	371.51	369.69	368.18	366.87	366.94	368.27	369.62	369.40
2001	370.47	371.44	372.39	373.32	373.77	373.13	371.51	369.59	368.12	368.38	369.64	371.11	371.07
2002	372.38	373.08	373.87	374.93	375.58	375.44	373.91	371.77	370.72	370.50	372.19	373.71	373.17
2003	374.92	375.63	376.51	377.75	378.54	378.21	376.65	374.28	373.12	373.10	374.67	375.97	375.78
2004	377.03	377.87	378.88	380.42	380.62	379.66	377.48	376.07	374.10	374.47	376.15	377.51	377.52

(continued)

Year	Jan	Feb	Mar	Apr	May	Jun	Jul	Aug	Sep	Oct	Nov	Dec	Annual
2005	378.43	379.70	380.91	382.20	382.45	382.14	380.60	378.60	376.72	376.98	378.29	380.07	379.76
2006	381.36	382.19	382.65	384.65	384.94	384.01	382.15	380.33	378.81	379.06	380.17	381.85	381.85
2007	382.88	383.77	384.42	386.36	386.53	386.01	384.45	381.96	380.81	381.09	382.37	383.84	383.71
2008	385.42	385.72	385.96	387.18	388.50	387.88	386.38	384.15	383.07	382.98	384.11	385.54	385.57
2009	386.92	387.41	388.77	389.46	390.18	389.43	387.74	385.91	384.77	384.38	385.99	387.27	387.35
2010	388.54	389.87	391.07	392.46	392.96	392.03	390.10	388.15	386.80	387.17			

*From http://co2now.org/index.php?option=com_content&task=view&id=22&Itemid=1

 **Observations**

1. Was there an increase or decrease in carbon dioxide levels over a 20-year period?

2. Why do you think there was an increase?

3. How does a rise in carbon dioxide levels affect temperatures on Earth?

4. How does a change in temperature result in climate change?

Our Findings

Please refer to the Our Findings appendix at the back of this volume.

Further Reading

"Climate Change." *EPA*, 2010. Available online. URL: http://www. epa.gov/climatechange/. Accessed April 24, 2010. Links on the EPA's official Web site to facts about global warming and climate change.

————. *The Oxford Companion to Ships and the Sea*. 2006. Available online. URL: http://www.encyclopedia.com/doc/10225-climatechange.html. Accessed April 24, 2010. Concise explanation of climate change in a short encyclopedia entry.

Henson, Robert. *The Rough Guide to Climate Change*, 2nd ed. London: Rough Guides, 2008. Simplified scientific information explaining what climate change is, why it is happening, and its impact on the Earth.

Kovats, R. Sari. "Climate Change and Human Health." *Encyclopedia of Public Health*. 2002. Available online. URL: http://www. encyclopedia.com/doc/1G2-3404000189.html. Accessed April 24, 2010. Discusses the impact of climate change on public health.

Schmidt, Gavin, and Joshua Wolfe. *Climate Change: Picturing the Science*. New York: W.W. Norton & Company, 2009. Photojournal of the changes that have occurred across the globe due to climate change and global warming.

7. GEOLOGIC TIME SCALE

Introduction

The *geologic time scale* is a *chronological* model relating *stratigraphy* to the timing between events that occurred on Earth. Some of the types of events used to find relationships in time include *mass extinctions*, differences in rock layers, and the presence of certain types of *fossils*. The time line is broken down into units of time, with the largest unit being the *supereon*, which is made up of *eons*. Eons can then be further divided into *eras*, which are composed of *epochs*, which can be divided into *ages*. The first published geologic time scale was authored by Arthur Holmes (1890–1965), a British *geologist*. Back in 1913 when he created that time scale, he proposed the Earth's age to be 1.6 billion years. Today, we believe that number to be about 4.6 billion years.

In this activity, you will create a model of the geologic time scale by converting the units of time to a distance scale.

Time Needed

2 to 3 hours

What You Need

- colored pencils
- meterstick
- ruler (metric)
- rolls of paper used for calculators or cash registers, about 15 feet total (5 meters)

✎ transparent tape

✎ scissors

 ## Safety Precautions

Please review and follow the safety guidelines at the beginning of this volume.

What You Do

Using the information from Data Table 1 (based on a table from http://oceans1.csusb.edu/, accessed April 27, 2010), convert the times provided in Data Table 2 from years to distance units.

Data Table 1						
Time		**Distance**				
1 GA	=	1 m	or	100 cm	or	1,000 mm
100 MA	=	0.1 m	or	10 cm	or	100 mm
10 MA	=	0.01 m	or	1 cm	or	10 mm
1 MA	=	0.001 m	or	0.1 cm	or	1 mm
100,000 yr	=	0.0001 m	or	0.01 cm	or	0.1 mm
10,000 yr	=	0.00001 m	or	0.001 cm	or	0.01 mm
1,000 yr	=	0.000001 m	or	0.0001 cm	or	0.001 mm

Key: GA = billion years; MA = million years.

Data Table 2			
Event	Time intervals: time before present GA = billion years; MA = million years	Calculate the distance on the time line	
		Beginning	End
Precambrian Time	4.6 GA to 544 MA		
Proterozoic Era	2.5 GA to 544 MA		
Vendian Period	544 MA to 650 MA		
Cambrian Period	544 MA to 505 MA		
Paleozoic Era	544 MA to 248 MA		
Phanerozoic Eon	544 MA to present		
Ordovician Period	505 MA to 440 MA		
Silurian Period	440 MA to 410 MA		
Devonian Period	410 MA to 360 MA		
Carboniferous Period	360 MA to 286 MA		
Permian Period	286 MA to 248 MA		
Triassic Period	248 MA to 213 MA		
Mesozoic Era	248 MA to 65 MA		
Jurassic Period	213 MA to 145 MA		
Cretaceous Period	145 MA to 65 MA		

(continued)

Paleocene Epoch	65 MA to 55.5 MA		
Tertiary Period	65 MA to 1.8 MA		
Cenozoic Era	65 MA to present		
Eocene Epoch	55.5 MA to 33.7 MA		
Oligocene Epoch	33.7 MA to 23.8 MA		
Milocene Epoch	23.8 MA to 5.3 MA		
Pliocene Epoch	5.3 MA to 1.8 MA		
Pleistocene Epoch	1.8 MA to 8,000 years ago		
Quaternary Period	1.8 MA to present		
Holocene Epoch	8,000 years ago to present		

Fossil record

Event	Time before present	Time unit	Calculate the distance on the time line
Early bacteria and algae	3.4	GA	
First animal evidence (jellyfish)	1.2	GA	
Early multicelled organisms	700	MA	
First animals with backbones	500	MA	
First fish	490	MA	
Early land plants	430	MA	

(continued)

First amphibians	400	MA	
First reptiles	325	MA	
First dinosaurs	245	MA	
Early birds and mammals	180	MA	
Early flowering plants	150	MA	
Dinosaurs became extinct	65	MA	
Early primates	60	MA	

Human existence

Event	Time before present	Time unit	Calculate the distance on the time line
Australopithecus	3	MA	
Homo erectus	1.3	MA	
Neanderthal man	100,000	years	
Modern man	10,000	years	

Recent human events

Event	Date present	Years ago	Calculate the distance on the time line
Mount Vesuvius destroys Pompeii	79 CE		
First man on the moon	1969		

(continued)

First U.S. satellite orbited	1958		
Your birth date			

1. Starting with Precambrian time, 4.6 billion years ago, plot this time interval onto the roll of paper. That is the furthest back the time line goes, so you will know how long a piece of paper you need. If you run out of paper on one roll, tape the end to the next roll and continue working.

2. Continue to plot geologic events. Make sure to label them. For events that last over a period of time and are not just at one point in time, make sure to connect the beginning and end of the intervals with a line.

3. Plot on the paper the fossil record, human existence, and more recent human events. For points in time, a single point on the paper is fine. You can use different colors to represent different types of events.

 **Observations**

1. How does the time of human existence and events compare to the rest of the geologic time scale?
2. What information can you learn from the geologic time scale?
3. What information did scientists use to create a geologic scale?

Our Findings

Please refer to the Our Findings appendix at the back of this volume.

Further Reading

"Geologic Time Scale." Geology.com, 2010. Available online. URL: http://geology.com/time.htm. Accessed April 27, 2010. Includes a version of the geologic time scale that shows only the time intervals and has numerous links to related articles.

————. *The Columbia Encyclopedia*, 6th ed. 2008. Available online. URL: http://www.encyclopedia.com/doc/1E1-geolog-ts.html. Accessed April 27, 2010. A concise definition of the time scale along with a link to another image of the time scale.

Mehling, Randy. *Great Extinctions of the Past (Scientific American)* . New York: Chelsea House Publishers, 2007. Young adult book with information about the various mass extinctions that are documented in the fossil record.

Parks, Peggy. *The Extinction of the Dinosaurs*. Farmington Hills, MI: KidHaven Press, 2007. Children's book that provides simple explanations of the theories about what caused the extinction of dinosaurs.

"What Is Geologic Time?" USGS, 2010. Available online. URL: http://www.nature.nps.gov/geology/usgsnps/gtime/gtime1.html. Accessed April 27, 2010. Explains how scientists developed the time scale and provides examples to help understand the proportions of time involved.

8. GREENHOUSE GASES

Introduction

The *greenhouse effect* is the warming of the Earth due to the presence of certain gases in the atmosphere that absorb and *emit radiation*. *Greenhouse gases* include *water vapor*, *carbon dioxide*, *methane*, and *ozone*. Without these gases, the Earth would be much colder. However, many scientists believe that the burning of *fossil fuels* over many decades has caused an increase in some of these greenhouse gases, mainly carbon dioxide, which in turn has caused an increase in temperatures around the planet. The rise in temperature then results in *climate change*, which impacts *habitats* and wildlife. Because of mounting evidence demonstrating that climate change is occurring, many countries have adopted *regulations* for lowering greenhouse gas *emissions*.

In this experiment, you will simulate different atmospheric gases and compare their effects on air temperature.

Time Needed

15 minutes to prepare, 1 hour to complete

What You Need

- ✎ 2 empty 2-liter bottles
- ✎ 2 cans of carbonated soda, such as Coca-Cola®
- ✎ 2 stoppers (that fit the opening of a 2-liter bottle) with holes
- ✎ 2 thermometers

- small lump of modeling clay
- pencil
- 2 labels
- black marker
- sunny area
- clock or timer

Safety Precautions

Please review and follow the safety guidelines at the beginning of this volume.

What You Do

1. Insert each of the 2 thermometers into a stopper (Figure 1).

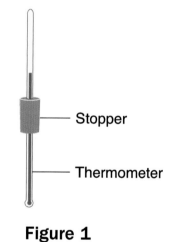

Stopper

Thermometer

Figure 1

2. Shake a can of carbonated soda.
3. Carefully open the soda, so that it does not spill. (Figure 2).

Figure 2

4. Once all the gas has been released, pour the gas-free soda into an empty 2-liter bottle.

5. Seal the bottle with a stopper (Figure 3).

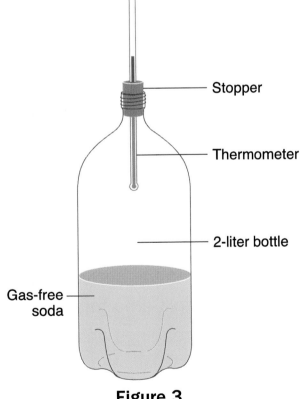

Figure 3

6. Label the bottle "nitrogen/oxygen," as the gases left in the bottle are mostly those in the air around you, which are primarily nitrogen and oxygen.

7. Being careful not to shake it, open the second can of soda and quickly pour the contents into the other bottle.

8. Quickly place a stopper in the bottle.

9. Swirl the contents of the bottle to release the carbonation, and try to avoid wetting the thermometer, although the experiment will not be spoiled if the thermometer becomes wet (Figure 4).

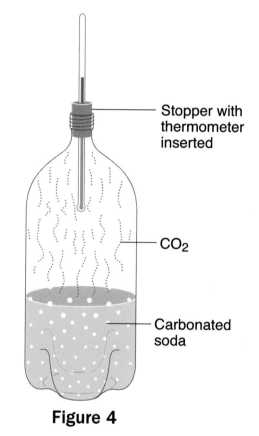

Stopper with thermometer inserted

CO_2

Carbonated soda

Figure 4

10. Label this bottle "CO_2" (carbon dioxide); the carbonation you released from the soda into the bottle is carbon dioxide.

11. Place both bottles in a sunlit area for about an hour.

12. After the hour, check the readings on the 2 thermometers.

 **Observations**

1. Was there a difference in the thermometer readings of the 2 bottles? If so, which had the higher reading?

2. What was the purpose of releasing the carbonation from one can before pouring it into the bottle but not doing so with the other can?

3. How does this experiment simulate the effect of greenhouse gases?

4. How do you think greenhouse gases might affect the Earth?

Our Findings

Please refer to the Our Findings appendix at the back of this volume.

Further Reading

Environmental Protection Agency. "Greenhouse Gas Emissions." *EPA.gov*. Available online. URL: http://www.epa.gov/climatechange/emissions/index.html. Accessed April 22, 2010. This official Web site of the EPA provides information defining greenhouse gases along with links to additional, related information.

"Greenhouse Effect." *UXL Encyclopedia of Science*. 2002. Available online. URL: http://www.encyclopedia.com/doc/1G2-3438100336.html. Accessed April 22, 2010. Long encyclopedia entry detailing greenhouse gases, the greenhouse effect, and related definitions.

"Greenhouse Gas News." Greenhouse Gas Online. Available online. URL: http://www.ghgonline.org/. Accessed April 22, 2010. Web site with frequently updated information includes links to greenhouse gas in the news.

Silver, Jerry. *Global Warming and Climate Change Demystified*. New York: McGraw-Hill, 2008. Includes a review of the current data and evidence for the effects of greenhouse gases on the Earth.

Tanaka, Shelley. *Climate Change*. Toronto: Groundwood Books, 2006. This book for young adults explains climate change and its threat to the planet.

9. CREATING LIGHTNING

Introduction

Lightning is the *discharge* of *electricity* that occurs during a *thunderstorm*. Lightning has also been known to form during *volcanic eruptions* and dust storms. Lightning can travel 60,000 meters per second and can reach temperatures as high as 30,000 degrees Celsius (54,000 degrees Fahrenheit). The most common type of lightning is cloud-to-ground lightning in which there is an electrical discharge from a *cumulonimbus* cloud to the ground. Since light travels faster than sound, the accompanying thunder occurs after the lightning strike. Despite the fact that lightning is generated during storms, there are several ways in which electrical energy can be built up and then discharged: for example, in the form of a spark or small bolt of lightning.

In this experiment, you will build up an electrical charge and release it in a form that simulates a small lightning bolt.

Time Needed

20 minutes

What You Need

- ✎ large sheet of plastic (e.g., a plastic clothing cover from a dry cleaner)
- ✎ rubber gloves
- ✎ steel pot with a plastic handle (aluminum pots will not work)

iron or steel fork

 table

 tape, any type

 room that can be darkened

 partner to operate the light switch

 timer, clock, or watch

Safety Precautions

Please review and follow the safety guidelines at the beginning of this volume. Stay alert to avoid electric shock.

What You Do

1. Lay the plastic sheet over the table.
2. Tape the plastic sheet to the table so that it does not move (Figure 1).

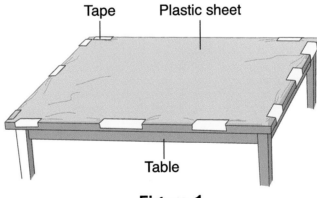

Tape   Plastic sheet

Table

Figure 1

3. Put on the rubber gloves.
4. Hold the pot by the handle.
5. Rub the pot back and forth over the plastic (Figure 2) for about 30 seconds.

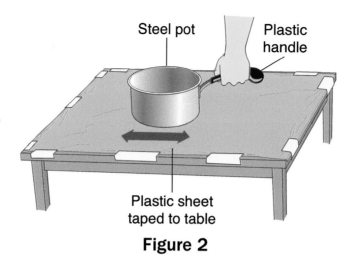

Steel pot

Plastic handle

Plastic sheet taped to table

Figure 2

6. Immediately have your friend darken the room.

7. While still holding the pot handle in one hand, hold the steel fork in the other hand.

8. Move the fork toward the pot (Figure 3). When the fork is about 1/2 inch away from the pot, you will see a spark.

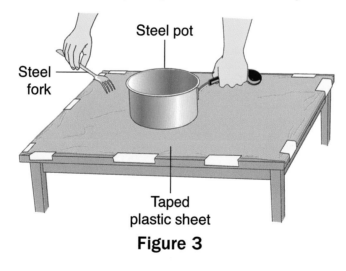

Steel pot

Steel fork

Taped plastic sheet

Figure 3

 **Observations**

1. Describe what you observed.

2. How does the build-up of electricity you created relate to lightning during a storm?

3. Why did you have to wear rubber gloves and hold the plastic handle of the pot?

Our Findings

Please refer to the Our Findings appendix at the back of this volume.

Further Reading

"(The) Electric Ben Franklin." *U.S.History.org*, 2010. Available online. URL: http://www.ushistory.org/franklin/info/kite.htm. Accessed April 24, 2010. Web site contains several articles and essays about the famous lightning-and-kite experiment performed by Benjamin Franklin.

Friedman, John. *Out of the Blue: A History of Lightning*. Brooklyn, NY: Delta, 2009. Provides facts about lightning, personal accounts of people being hit or witnessing lightning, as well as superstitions surrounding lightning strikes.

"Lightning." *National Geographic*, 2010. Available online. URL: http://environment.nationalgeographic.com/environment/natural-disasters/lightning-profile.html. Accessed April 24, 2010. Provides photos and facts about lightning.

———. *The Columbia Encyclopedia,* 6th ed. *2008.* Available online. URL: http://www.encyclopedia.com/doc/1E1-lightnin.html. Accessed April 24, 2010. Short entry explaining how lightning occurs.

Mayer, Cassie. *Thunder and Lightning*. Mankato, MN: Heinemann-Raintree, 2007. Children's book explaining what thunder and lightning are.

10. SMOG

Introduction

Photochemical smog, commonly known simply as smog, is produced through a series of photochemical *reactions* with *volatile organic compounds*, *nitrogen oxide*, and sunlight. The result includes *particulate matter* and a form of *ozone*. Smog is mainly generated from *pollution* caused by car and industrial *emissions*, as well as by the burning of coal. Though smog is most common in areas with a lot of automobile traffic and a sunny, dry climate, it can be carried by the wind to other areas. Smog is harmful to human health, especially for the elderly, those with heart problems, people with *respiratory* issues, and children. Smog can cause *wheezing*, coughing, and shortness of breath. Some areas tend to *accumulate* smog more readily than others, not just because of the amount of pollution but also because areas with warm upper air can trap the smog and prevent it from *dissipating*.

In this experiment, you will recreate the conditions for creating smog and observe how smog can become trapped in a location.

Time Needed

40 minutes

What You Need

- ✎ shoebox, no lid
- ✎ 2 paper towel cardboard tubes
- ✎ lump of modeling clay
- ✎ candle

2 matches, about 8 in. long

  plastic wrap, enough to cover the shoebox

  roll of transparent tape

  paper towel, 1 sheet

  scissors

  pencil

  clock or timer

Safety Precautions

Please review and follow the safety guidelines at the beginning of this volume. Adult supervision is required during this experiment. Always exercise caution when working near flames, and have a fire extinguisher nearby.

What You Do

1. Turn the shoebox upside down, and place the end of a paper towel tube toward one end of the long side of the shoebox. With a pencil, trace around it (Figure 1).

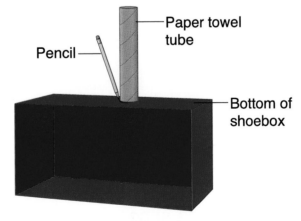

Figure 1

2. Move the paper towel tube a few inches away and repeat step 1.

3. With the scissors, cut out the 2 circles that you drew.

4. Stick the paper towel tubes down into the holes you cut out, and tape them in place so that there are no spaces between the tubes and the shoebox (Figure 2). The tubes should extend about 2 in. into the box.

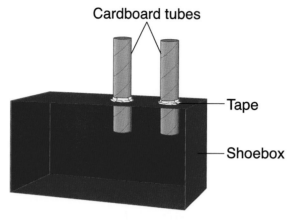

Figure 2

5. Stick the lump of clay directly under one of the tubes.

6. Place the candle into the clay so that the candle is held in place. The top of the candle wick should be at least 2 in. below the tube (Figure 3).

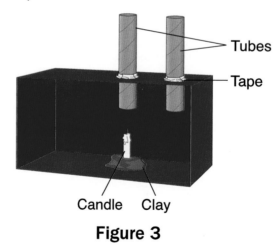

Figure 3

7. Cover the open side of the shoebox with plastic wrap (Figure 4).

8. Tape the plastic wrap in place all around the box so that there are no openings (Figure 4).

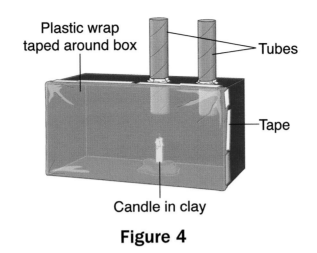

Plastic wrap
taped around box

Tubes

Tape

Candle in clay

Figure 4

9. Light one of the long matches and carefully insert it into the tube under which the candle was placed. Light the candle. Be careful not to burn yourself or set on fire the shoebox or paper towel tubes.

10. Blow out the match

11. Wait about 5 minutes.

12. Crumple the paper towel.

13. Strike another match and light the paper towel. (Be careful not to burn yourself!)

14. Blow out the flames after 5 seconds, leaving the paper towel smoking.

15. Hold the smoking paper towel over the tube that does not have the candle under it.

16. Observe what happens to the smoke.

 **Observations**

1. What happened to the smoke?

2. Why did the smoke remain in the box?

3. How does this simulate photochemical smog?

4. Why would it be unhealthy to stay outdoors when there is smog?

Our Findings

Please refer to the Our Findings appendix at the back of this volume.

Further Reading

"Local Air Quality Conditions and Forecasts." AIRNow, 2010. Available online. URL: http://www.airnow.gov/. Accessed April 30, 2010. Web site with up-to-date air quality information around the United States.

Rapp, Valerie. *Protecting Earth's Air Quality (Saving Our Living Earth)*. Minneapolis, MN: Lerner Publications, 2008. Book for upper-elementary students explaining the dangers of air pollution and what needs to be done to improve air quality.

"Smog." *The Columbia Encyclopedia*, 6th ed. 2008. Available online. URL: http://www.encyclopedia.com/doc/1E1-smog.html. Accessed April 30, 2010. Brief entry that explains how smog is formed and trapped.

"South Coast Air Quality Management District." South Coast AQMD, 2010. Available online. URL: http://www.aqmd.gov/. Accessed April 30, 2010. Web site with information for the smoggiest counties in the United States, located in Southern California.

Wise, William. *Killer Smog: The World's Worst Air Pollution Disaster*. Bloomington, IN: iUniverse, 2001. Provides details about the famous London smog in the 1950s that caused thousands of deaths and relates this information to our air pollution issues today.

11. WEATHERING

Introduction

Weathering refers to the breaking down of rocks from exposure to Earth's *atmospheric* conditions. Weathering should not be confused with *erosion*, which not only includes the weathering of rocks but also encompasses the impact or transport of rock or debris by wind, ice, water, gravity, and living organisms. *Physical weathering*, also known as *mechanical weathering*, is the breakdown of rocks due to such atmospheric conditions as ice, water, heat, and *pressure*. Another type of weathering is *chemical weathering*, which is the breakdown of rocks from biological or chemical *agents*. Examples include *oxidation* and the effects of *acid* found in acid rain (as opposed to the effect of the rain itself).

In this activity, you will simulate the effects of weathering and observe the results.

Time Needed

10 minutes to prepare
1 week to complete

What You Need

- 2 handfuls of clay
- plastic wrap, enough to wrap each piece of clay completely
- freezer
- flat surface in a sunny area
- pencil

Safety Precautions

Please review and follow the safety guidelines at the beginning of this volume.

What You Do

1. Try to make sure that the 2 lumps of clay are about equal in size.

2. Using your hands, roll both pieces of clay into round balls (Figure 1).

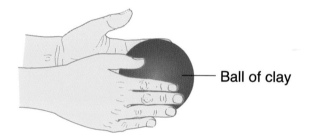

Ball of clay

Figure 1

3. Observe the 2 pieces of clay, and sketch what you observe on the data table.

4. Wrap each ball of clay completely in plastic wrap.

5. Place 1 ball of clay in the freezer.

6. Leave the other ball on a flat surface in a sunny area.

7. After 24 hours, remove both pieces of clay from the plastic wrap.

8. Observe both pieces of clay and sketch what you observed on the data table.

9. Rewrap both pieces and return them to their respective areas (freezer and sunny area).

10. Repeat steps 7 to 9 each day until you have done so for a week.

Data Table		
Day	**Sketch of frozen clay**	**Sketch of clay from sunny area**
1		
2		
3		
4		
5		
6		
7		

 **Observations**

1. What major difference did you observe between the 2 pieces of clay after 1 day?
2. Did the differences continue to become more apparent after several days?
3. How does this simulate weathering of rocks?
4. What are some other conditions to which you might subject the clay that would simulate weathering?

Our Findings

Please refer to the Our Findings appendix at the back of this volume.

Further Reading

Allaby, Alisa, and Michael Allaby. "Chemical Weathering." *A Dictionary of Earth Sciences*. 1999. Available online. URL: http://www. encyclopedia.com/doc/1O13-chemicalweathering.html. Accessed April 30, 2010. Brief entry that defines chemical weathering as opposed to physical weathering.

Gifford, Clive. *Weathering and Erosion*. Mankato, MN: Smart Apple Media, 2005. Book for upper-elementary-age students that explains the processes involved in both weathering and erosion.

Mattern, Joanne. *Weathering and Erosion and the Rock Cycle*. New York: Powerkids Press, 2005. Book for upper-elementary-age students that details the rock cycle, along with the impact of weathering on rocks.

"Weather." *The Columbia Encyclopedia*, 6th ed. 2008. Available online. URL: http://www.encyclopedia.com/doc/1E1-weather.html. Accessed April 30, 2010. Entry explaining what weather conditions are and how the weather is measured.

"Weathering." *The Columbia Encyclopedia*, 6th ed. 2008. Available online. URL: http://www.encyclopedia.com/doc/1E1-weatheri.html. Accessed April 30, 2010. Entry that concisely explains the process of rock disintegration due to atmospheric conditions.

12. PLATE BOUNDARIES

Introduction

Plate boundaries are found at the edges of the plates of the *lithosphere*, which is made up of the Earth's *crust* and the upper *mantle*. There are 3 types of plate boundaries that exist: *convergent*, *divergent*, and *transform*. Convergent boundaries are where the giant plates are pushed together. Divergent boundaries are where plates are pulling away from each other. Transform boundaries are where plates slide horizontally past each other. *Subduction zones* and *continental collisions* are typical of convergent boundaries. *Mid-ocean ridges* are common along divergent boundaries, such as the Mid-Atlantic Ridge. Finally, earthquake *faults* are common at transform boundaries, such as the San Andreas Fault located in California.

In this activity, you will plot earthquake activity from the prior week and use that information to deduce where there are likely to be plate boundaries.

Time Needed

45 minutes

What You Need

- ✐ 5 pencils of different colors
- ✐ computer with Internet access

Safety Precautions

Please review and follow the safety guidelines at the beginning of this volume.

What You Do

1. Visit the United States Geological Service Web site at http://neic.usgs.gov/neis/qed/.

2. Find information regarding earthquake activity for the previous week.

3. Show on the data table, for each of 5 days, the date, magnitude, latitude, and longitude for 8 to 10 earthquakes a day of magnitude 3.0 or larger.

4. Using the information on your data table, plot the earthquakes on the map in Figure 1 by finding the correct latitude and longitude. Use a different colored pencil for each different date.

5. Observe your map

Data Table			
Date	Magnitude	Latitude	Longitude

(continued)

Date	Magnitude	Latitude	Longitude

(continued)

Date	Magnitude	Latitude	Longitude

Date	Magnitude	Latitude	Longitude

(continued)

Date	Magnitude	Latitude	Longitude

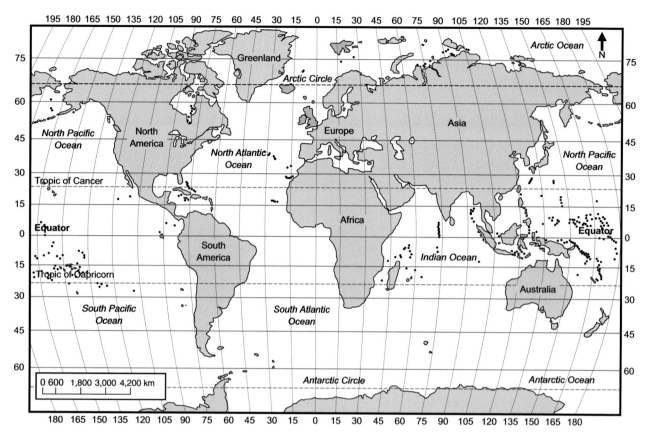

Figure 1. Map of the world, adapted from http://www.mapsofworld.com/ world-map-2008.jpg

 **Observations**

1. Were there earthquakes in the same regions of the world on more than 1 day of the week? If so, where?

2. Is there ever a day without an earthquake? Explain why or why not.

3. Based on your plotted map, where do you think there are plate boundaries? Draw a line where you think they exist.

Our Findings

Please refer to the Our Findings appendix at the back of this volume.

Further Reading

Kusky, Timothy. *Earthquakes: Plate Tectonics and Earthquake Hazards*. New York: Facts On File, 2008. An explanation of how earthquakes occur, including background information on the theory of plate tectonics and what occurs at plate boundaries.

Nardo, Don. *Plate Tectonics*. San Diego, CA: Lucent, 2003. Young adult-level book explaining the theory of plate tectonics and the resulting occurrences on the Earth.

"Plate Boundaries." Jet Propulsion Laboratory, 2010. Available online. URL: http://scign.jpl.nasa.gov/learn/plate4.htm. Accessed April 27, 2010. Provides details and diagrams about different types of plate boundaries.

"Plate Tectonics." Platetectonics.com, 2010. Available online. URL: http://www.platetectonics.com/book/page_5.asp. Accessed April 27, 2010. Provides definitions of the different types of plate boundaries, along with diagrams of each.

"San Andreas Fault." *The Columbia Encyclopedia*, 6th ed. 2008. Available online. URL: http://www.encyclopedia.com/doc/1E1-SanAndre.html. Accessed April 27, 2010. Information about one of the most famous faults, the San Andreas, located in California, which gives rise to major earthquakes.

13. BUILDING A HELE-SHAW CELL

Introduction

The *Hele-Shaw cell* was named after the British automobile engineer Henry Selby Hele-Shaw (1854–1941). He was known for many achievements, including his experiments with fluids and thin *cells*, named in his honor. The purpose of a Hele-Shaw cell is to view a two-dimensional representation of what would otherwise be a three-dimensional occurrence, usually for observing the *properties* of *viscous liquids* but also for observing patterns in *sediment deposition*.

In this activity, you will build your own Hele-Shaw cell and be able to use it in future experiments.

Time Needed

25 minutes

What You Need

- clear CD (compact disc) or DVD case
- 3 wooden pencils
- pencil sharpener
- plastic funnel
- masking tape, a few pieces
- ruler

Safety Precautions

Please review and follow the safety guidelines at the beginning of this volume.

What You Do

1. Open the CD case.

2. Remove any paper inserts.

3. If there are any holes in the back of the case, tape them over with masking tape.

4. Remove the top cover of the case from its hinges (Figure 1).

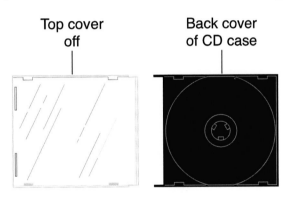

Figure 1

5. Flip both the front and back cover over and place them back to back so that the flat side of each faces the other (Figure 2).

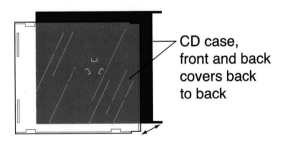

Figure 2

6. Slide a pencil in between the 2 case pieces at the very bottom, and tape the pencil in place (Figure 3).

CD covers

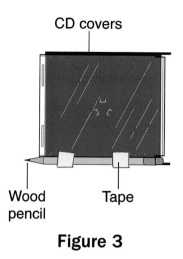

Wood   Tape
pencil

Figure 3

7. Sharpen 1 pencil so that it is the height of the CD case.

8. Place this pencil in between the CD case covers, on the side opposite where the hinges were, and tape the pencil in place (Figure 4).

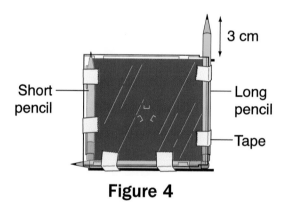

3 cm

Short ——   —— Long
pencil   pencil

                                    —— Tape

Figure 4

9. Sharpen the other pencil so that it sticks up about 3 cm longer than the height of the CD case.

10. Place this pencil in between the CD case covers where the hinges were and tape the pencil in place (Figure 4).

11. With masking tape, completely cover the bottom edge and the side edges where the pencils are so that there are no open spaces except on top, where there is no pencil (Figure 5).

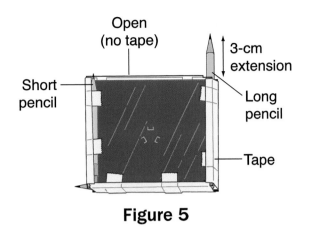

Figure 5

12. Place the funnel just to the inside of the pencil that is sticking up so that the end of the funnel is in between the 2 CD cover pieces (Figure 6). Tape the funnel in place.

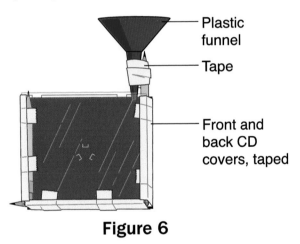

Figure 6

13. Your Hele-Shaw cell is ready!

 **Observations**

1. Why do we want to create a space between the 2 CD cover pieces?

2. Why do we keep that space narrow?

3. What could you use this device to test?

Our Findings

Please refer to the Our Findings appendix at the back of this volume.

Further Reading

eFluids.com. 2010. Available online. URL: http://www.efluids.com/. Accessed April 29, 2010. Links to sites about fluid mechanics and fluid dynamics.

"Fluid Mechanics." *The Columbia Encyclopedia*, 6th ed. 2008. Available online. URL: http://www.encyclopedia.com/doc/1E1-fluidmec.html. Accessed April 29, 2010. Short entry explaining fluid mechanics.

Kusky, Timothy. *Encyclopedia of Earth Science*. New York: Facts On File, 2004. High school-level reading providing a comprehensive reference for earth science topics.

Pierre Y., Julien. *Erosion and Sedimentation*. New York: Cambridge University Press, 2010. Basic textbook, updated, that thoroughly explains how erosion and sedimentation occur.

Rezanezhad, Fereidoun. *Experimental Study of Fingering Flow in Porous Hele-Shaw Cells*. Saarbrücken, Germany: VDM Verlag, 2008. Advanced reading about scientific research regarding the path that sediments follow as water and solutes travel through various media.

Walker, Sally. *Secrets of a Civil War Submarine: Solving the Mysteries of the H. L. Hunley*. Minneapolis, MN. Carolrhoda Books, 2005. True story of a submarine built by the Confederates during the Civil War, how it was found, and how its fate was presumed to have occurred based on water flow and sediment deposition.

14. USING A HELE-SHAW CELL

Introduction

Sedimentation is the tendency of *sediments* or *particles* that are suspended in water or some liquid to settle. These sediments build up over time, either at the bottom of a body of water or along the sides where there is *solid matter*, though different materials tend to build up at different angles rather than settle evenly. The *deposition* of sediments over time creates *sedimentary rocks*. One branch of *geology*, called *stratigraphy*, is dedicated to the study of rock layers. Geologists learn about rocks from the layering of sedimentary rocks. These layers actually build up three-dimensionally, so when we look at a two-dimensional *cross section*, we do not see the entire picture. However, with the help of a *Hele-Shaw cell*, we can view in two dimensions what is actually occurring during the sedimentation process.

In this activity, you will use a Hele-Shaw cell to study patterns in sedimentation and stratigraphy.

Time Needed

60 minutes

What You Need

- Hele-Shaw cell (see Experiment 13)
- index card
- protractor
- transparent tape, a few pieces

1/4 cup (50 ml) sand

 1/4 cup (50 ml) salt

 1/4 cup (50 ml) sugar

 1/4 cup (50 ml) rice

 1/4 cup (50 ml) lentils

 flat surface, such as a tabletop

 pen or pencil

Safety Precautions

Please review and follow the safety guidelines at the beginning of this volume.

What You Do

1. Hold the Hele-Shaw cell upright on the table (Figure 1).

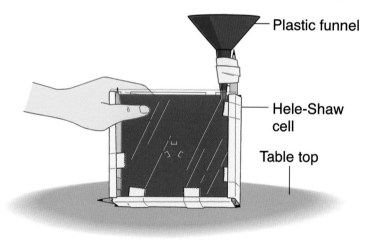

Figure 1

2. Pour 1/4 cup of sand into the funnel, without moving the Hele-Shaw cell.

3. Observe how the sand does not fill in the space evenly but, instead, has a slope.

4. Tape an index card to the outside of the cell so that the bottom edge of the card matches the slope of the sand while the bottom corner of the card touches the tabletop (Figure 2).

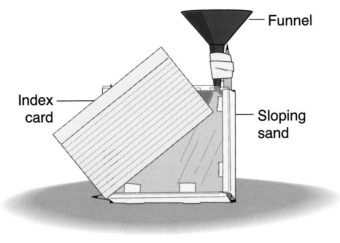

Figure 2

5. Set the protractor on the tabletop in front of the cell so that the bottom corner of the index card matches up with the center point of the protractor (Figure 3).

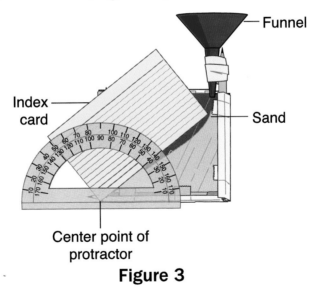

Figure 3

6. Use the protractor to measure the angle of repose (Figure 3).
7. Record the angle on the data table.
8. Remove the index card.
9. Pour the sand out of the cell.

10. Repeat steps 1 to 9 two more times.

11. Find the average angle of repose for sand.

12. Repeat steps 1 to 11 for salt, sugar, rice, and lentils.

Data Table				
Material	**Angle of repose, trial 1**	**Angle of repose, trial 2**	**Angle of repose, trial 3**	**Average Angle of repose (trials 1+2+3 divided by 3)**
Sand				
Salt				
Sugar				
Rice				
Lentils				

 **Observations**

1. Did all of the materials have the same angle of repose? Why or why not?

2. What was the benefit of checking the angle of repose for each material 3 times?

3. What do you think the angle of repose would be if you poured in a mixture of half sand and half salt? Why? (Test it and see if you were right.)

4. How does a Hele-Shaw cell help us understand patterns in sedimentation and stratigraphy?

Our Findings

Please refer to the Our Findings appendix at the back of this volume.

Further Reading

Faulkner, Rebecca. *Soil (Geology Rocks)* . Portsmouth, NH: Heinemann, 2008. This book contains detailed information at an upper-elementary reading level regarding rock formation and geological processes.

"Geology." USGS, 2010. Available online. URL: http://geology.usgs. gov/. Accessed April 30, 2010. Official government Web site with many links and abundant information on the field of geology.

Lambert, David. *The Field Guide to Geology*. New York: Checkmark Books, 2006. Young-adult version of a geology field guide, including diagrams explaining the processes that form rocks and sediments.

"Sediment." *The Columbia Encyclopedia*, 6th ed. 2008. Available online. URL: http://www.encyclopedia.com/doc/1E1-sediment. html. Accessed April 30, 2010. Entry that explains the makeup of sediments and how they are deposited.

"Stratigraphy." *The Columbia Encyclopedia*, 6th ed. 2008. Available online. URL: http://www.encyclopedia.com/doc/1E1-stratigr.html. Accessed April 30, 2010. Entry explaining the branch of geology known as stratigraphy.

15. THE ROCK CYCLE

Introduction

We often think of rocks as being with us forever. But rocks actually undergo many changes over long periods of time and can change their form. This transformation, known as the *rock cycle*, is a constant process. *Molten* rock, called *magma*, under the Earth's surface cools once it reaches the surface—a process known as *extrusion*—to form *igneous* rocks. Igneous rocks can undergo either *pressure* to form *metamorphic* rock or *erosion*, *deposition*, and *compaction*—part of a process known as *lithification*—to form *sedimentary* rock. Sedimentary rock, under pressure and heat, forms metamorphic rock, which can also undergo erosion, deposition, and compaction to form sedimentary rock. When sedimentary or metamorphic rock is forced down under the Earth's crust, it becomes molten but may once again reach the surface to cool and form igneous rock.

In this activity, you will simulate the processes involved in the rock cycle and create models of the 3 major types of rocks found in the rock cycle.

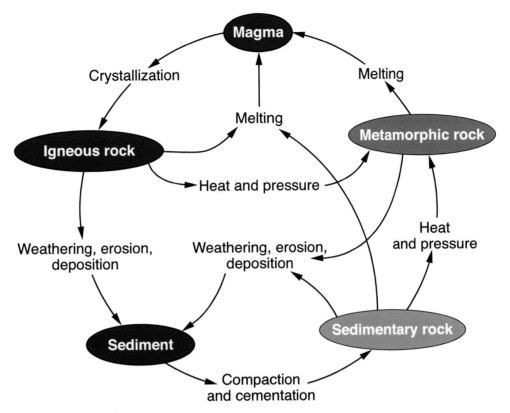

Figure 1. Transformation of rocks: the "rock cycle" (adapted from http://www.uwsp.edu/geo/faculty/ritter/geog101/textbook/earth_materials_structure/rock_cycle.html, accessed April 26, 2010).

Time Needed

45 to 60 minutes

What You Need

- 3 crayons, each a different color (e.g., Crayola®)
- 3 small paper plates
- plastic knife
- aluminum foil, about 6 in. x 6 in. (about 15 cm x 15 cm)
- Styrofoam® cup
- hot water, enough to fill the cup twice

Safety Precautions

Please review and follow the safety guidelines at the beginning of this volume. Adult supervision is recommended when heating water or handling hot water.

What You Do

1. Remove the paper wrapping from the 3 crayons.
2. Using the plastic knife, shave off pieces of 1 crayon onto a paper plate. Continue until you have turned most of the crayon into a pile of shavings (Figure 2).

Crayon   Plastic knife

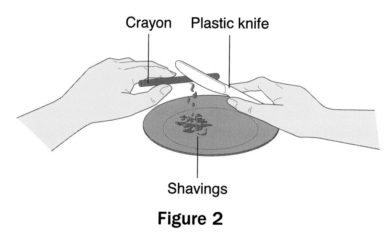

Shavings

Figure 2

3. Repeat step 2 with the other 2 crayons, making sure to place the shavings of each onto separate plates.
4. Pour the shavings from the first crayon onto the aluminum foil.
5. Fold up the aluminum foil over the shavings (Figure 3).

Aluminum foil

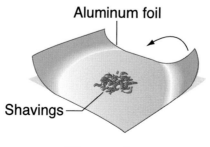

Shavings

Figure 3

6. Press down on the wrapped shavings to squeeze them together.

7. Carefully unwrap the foil.

8. Add the shavings from the second crayon on top of the (squeezed-together) first crayon shavings (Figure 4).

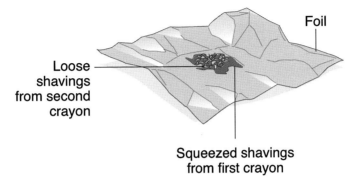

Foil

Loose
shavings
from second
crayon

Squeezed shavings
from first crayon

Figure 4

9. Repeat steps 5 to 7.

10. Repeat steps 8 and 9 with the shavings from the third crayon.

11. You now have a model of a sedimentary rock that is formed from the compaction of eroded sediments. Observe your model.

12. Remove the "rock" from the foil.

13. Fill the cup about 3/4 full with hot water.

14. Shape the foil so that it can hold the "rock" and float in the cup of water (Figure 5).

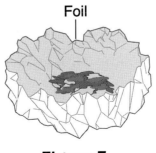

Foil

Figure 5

15. Place the foil, with the "rock" resting in it, into the cup of hot water (Figure 6).

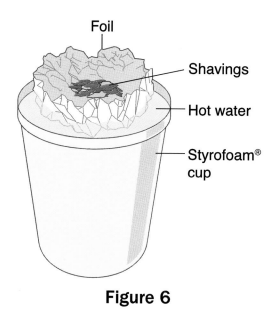

Foil

Shavings

Hot water

Styrofoam®
cup

Figure 6

16. When the crayon wax starts to soften and swirl, but not melt or mix completely, remove the foil and rock from the water.

17. You now have a model of a metamorphic rock formed from sedimentary rocks that have been subjected to heat and pressure. Observe your model.

18. Pour out the now-cooled water and refill the cup 3/4 full, once again with hot water.

19. Place your rock back into the foil and allow it to float in the hot water until the crayon wax melts completely and the colors blend.

20. You now have a model of an igneous rock that is formed from metamorphic rock melted under the Earth's surface at high temperatures, then cooling as it reaches the surface. Observe your model.

 **Observations**

1. What are some of the differences in the appearance of sedimentary, metamorphic, and igneous rocks?

2. What might happen to an igneous rock that would eventually cause pieces of it to end up in a sedimentary rock?

3. Why is it called the "rock cycle"?

Our Findings

Please refer to the Our Findings appendix at the back of this volume.

Further Reading

Faulkner, Rebecca. *Igneous Rock*. Sarasota, FL: Raintree, 2008. High-interest book geared toward young teens that explains how igneous rocks are formed and gives examples of the different types of igneous rocks.

————. *Sedimentary Rock*. Sarasota, FL: Raintree, 2007. For young teens, explains the process of sedimentary rock formation and has pictures of sedimentary rocks.

"The Rock Cycle." Rocksandminerals.com, 2005. Available online. URL: http://www.rocksandminerals.com/rockcycle.htm. Accessed April 26, 2010. Provides explanations and diagrams about the rock cycle and different types of rocks.

"Rocks." *UXL Encyclopedia of Science*. 2002. Available online. URL: http://www.encyclopedia.com/doc/1G2-3438100569.html. Accessed April 26, 2010. Explains the rock cycles and how all 3 types of rocks are formed.

"Rocks: Igneous, Metamorphic, and Sedimentary." Geology.com, 2010. Available online. URL: http://geology.com/rocks/. Accessed April 26, 2010. Contains photographs of all types of rocks, including details about each specific rock.

16. POROSITY OF ROCKS

Introduction

We think of rocks as *solid* objects, but they are not necessarily solid through and through. *Sedimentary rocks* are created when *erosion* occurs. With erosion, small pieces of earth are either washed downstream with water or blown by wind. They eventually settle and build up in layers. As *pressure* is added to these layers, sedimentary rocks are formed. When sedimentary rocks are formed in this manner, it follows that there must be small open spaces between the bits of earth and sand of which these rocks are *composed*. For example, *sandstone* is made of compressed layers of sand. Even when spaces in sandstone are too small to be seen without a *microscope*, these holes still exist. Depending on the *composition* of a rock, the porosity of rocks differ.

In this experiment, you will test the *porosity* of the materials from which sandstone is made.

Time Needed

40 minutes

What You Need

- gravel, 12 ounces (oz) (350 ml)
- sand, 12 oz
- silt, 12 oz
- 3 large beakers
- graduated cylinder, about 3.4 oz (100 ml)

✎ water, access to a faucet with running water is best

✎ 3 labels

✎ black marker

✎ calculator

Safety Precautions

Please review and follow the safety guidelines at the beginning of this volume.

What You Do

1. Fill 1 beaker to the 350-ml mark with gravel.

2. Label the beaker "Gravel" (Figure 1).

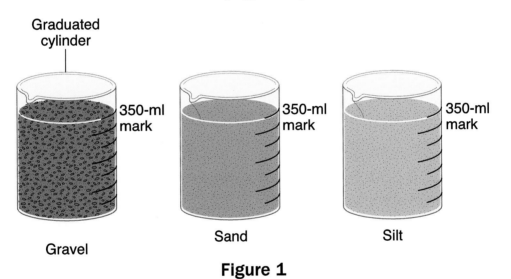

Graduated cylinder

350-ml mark

350-ml mark

350-ml mark

Gravel

Sand

Silt

Figure 1

3. Fill the second beaker to the 350-ml mark with sand.

4. Label the beaker "Sand" (Figure 1).

5. Fill the third beaker to the 350-ml mark with silt.

6. Label the beaker "Silt" (Figure 1).

7. Fill the graduated cylinder to the 100-ml mark.

8. Carefully pour water from the graduated cylinder into the beaker
    with the gravel until the water reaches the top of the gravel at
    the 350-ml mark (Figure 2). When you need more than 100 ml,
    fill the graduated cylinder to the 100-ml mark a second time,
    then continue pouring.

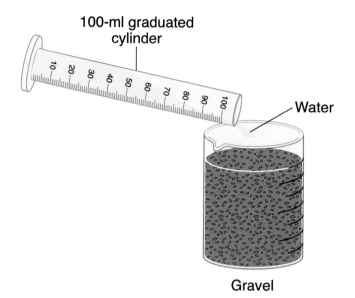

Figure 2

9. Note how much water is left in the graduated cylinder so that
    you can calculate the volume of water you poured into the
    beaker. For example, if you have 55 ml left and you started with
    100 ml, you poured 45 ml into the gravel. If you poured the
    entire contents of the cylinder into the gravel and then poured
    some from the cylinder a second time, make sure to add the
    first 100 ml you poured in!

10. Record on the data table the amount you poured into the gravel
    beaker.

11. Repeat steps 7 to 10 for the sand and the silt beakers.

12. Complete the data table.

Data Table			
Material	Volume of material	Volume of water poured into beaker	% Porosity = $\dfrac{\text{volume of water}}{\text{volume of material}} \times 100$
Gravel	350 ml		
Sand	350 ml		
Silt	350 ml		

 Observations

1. Which of the materials had the highest porosity?
2. Which of the materials had the lowest porosity?
3. If sandstone is made from these materials, do you think that sandstone is porous? Why or why not?
4. How do you think the characteristic of porosity might affect the weight of certain rocks?

Our Findings

Please refer to the Our Findings appendix at the back of this volume.

Further Reading

Adams, A. E., W. S. MacKenzie, and C. Guilford. *Atlas of Sedimentary Rocks Under the Microscope*. Hoboken, NJ: Wiley, 1984. Although this book is designed as a lab manual, it contains color photographs of cross sections of sedimentary rocks under the microscope so that the porosity of these rocks can be viewed.

Hancock, Paul, and Frian Skinner. "Permeability and Porosity." *The Oxford Companion to the Earth*. 2000. *Encyclopedia.com*. Available online. URL: http://www.encyclopedia.com/doc/10112-permeabilityandporosity.html. Accessed April 13, 2010. A detailed article about the porosity of a variety of materials.

"How Sedimentary Rock Is Formed." *Rock Hounds*, n.d. Available online. URL: http://www.fi.edu/fellows/fellow1/oct98/create/sediment.htm. Accessed April 13, 2010. Site explains in simple terms how sedimentary rocks are formed.

"Sedimentary Rocks." *Geology.com*, 2010. Available online. URL: http://geology.com/rocks/sedimentary-rocks.shtml. Accessed April 13, 2010. Site contains photographs and descriptions of different types of sedimentary rocks.

Stow, Dorrik. *Sedimentary Rocks in the Field: A Color Guide*. Salt Lake City, UT: Academic Press, 2005. Color photographs highlight this book for identifying sedimentary rocks.

17. MINING

Introduction

Mining is a term typically used to describe the *extraction* of valuable materials from the earth. Anything that cannot be grown or *manufactured* is likely to be mined. Examples of materials that are mined from the earth include *precious metals* (such as gold), metals in general, diamonds, and *uranium*. Materials can be extracted through sub-surface mining, i.e., mining that occurs underground. Most items, however, are mined by surface mining. Typically, mined materials are not in their pure form but are found as *ore*, a rock that contains precious materials. The value of the ore depends on how costly it is to separate out the desired precious materials from the rock as compared to the value of the precious materials. Unfortunately, mining can negatively impact the *environment* despite many of the *regulations* that have been put into place over the years. The mining industry deals also with safety issues.

In this activity, you will learn about mining by competing in a game with one or more friends.

Time Needed

20 minutes

What You Need

- 2 bags of chocolate chip cookies, 1 bag each from 2 different brands (Make sure that 1 brand has more chocolate chips per cookie than the other. Examples: Chips Ahoy® and Keebler's Chips Deluxe.®)

✎   graph paper, 1 sheet for each player

✎   flat toothpicks, 4 per player

✎   round toothpicks, 4 per player

✎   paper clips, 4 per player

✎   play money, $20 per player

✎   pencils, 1 for each player

✎   timer

Safety Precautions

Please review and follow the safety guidelines at the beginning of this volume.

What You Do

1. Pass out $20 in play money to each player, including yourself.

2. Hand out a sheet of graph paper to each player, including yourself.

3. The chocolate chip cookies represent pieces of land that can be "mined" for "previous" chocolate chips. Players must purchase a cookie. Refer to Data Table 1 for pricing.

4. When purchasing items, keep in mind that mining "equipment" will also be needed. Players may not touch the cookies directly during mining, so they will need to purchase "mining tools" like round or flat toothpicks and paper clips (see Data Table 1 for pricing).

5. Each player must place his or her cookies on a sheet of graph paper and trace the outline of the cookie.

6. The goal of the game is to pick out or "mine" as many chocolate chips as possible using the mining equipment (Figure 1).

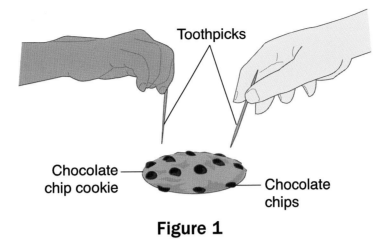

Figure 1

7. See Data Table 2 for game rules.

Data Table 1. Pricing	
Item	**Price**
Cookie with some chocolate chips	$5
Cookie with many chocolate chips	$7
Flat toothpick	$2
Round toothpick	$4
Paper clip	$6

Data Table 2. Game Rules
You cannot use your fingers to hold the cookie after it is traced. You must use the "mining tools."
If a mining tool breaks, it can no longer be used.
You can buy as many tools as you need.

(continued)

You have 5 minutes to mine your cookie.
Mining costs $1 per minute—any portion of a minute. If a full minute is not used, it is still charged as a full minute. Players may mine up to 5 minutes.
Players earn $2 per chocolate chip they mine. You can put together broken pieces of chips to make 1 chip.
You must clean up your mining area by making sure that all cookie pieces are within your outlined graph area before the 5 minutes are up. Until you have cleaned up, you are still being charged mining time at $1 per minute. You must use the mining tools to clean up.
The player who has cleaned up his or her mining area completely and has the most money wins.

 **Observations**

1. Was it easy to separate the chocolate chips from the cookie?
2. How does this separation relate to mining ore?
3. How does mining affect the environment? You can do additional research on this topic.

Our Findings

Please refer to the Our Findings appendix at the back of this volume.

Further Reading

"The California Gold Rush." Ceres. 2010. Available online. URL: http://ceres.ca.gov/ceres/calweb/geology/goldrush.html. Accessed April 20, 2010. Article from the California government Web site with a brief description of the California Gold Rush and related links.

"Coal Mining." *The Columbia Encyclopedia*, 6th ed. 2008. Available online. URL: http://www.encyclopedia.com/doc/1E1-coalmini.html. Accessed April 20, 2010. Article specific to how coal is mined and the dangers involved.

"Mining." *The Columbia Encyclopedia*, 6th ed. 2008. Available online. URL: http://www.encyclopedia.com/doc/1E1-mining.html. Accessed April 20, 2010. Article explaining the different materials that are mined and how they are mined.

Punke, Michael. *Fire and Brimstone: The North Butte Mining Disaster of 1917*. New York: Hyperion, 2007. Details the disaster at a copper mine where a fire broke out and more than 100 people died.

Raum, Elizabeth. *The California Gold Rush*. Mankato, MN: Capstone Press, 2008. Book for ages 9 to 12 about the California Gold Rush, where many people flocked in hopes of finding gold and striking it rich.

18. SOLAR SYSTEM

Introduction

Our *solar system* consists of a *star*, *planets*, *comets*, *asteroids*, and other bodies. The Inner Solar System is the area closest to the Sun and includes the planets Mercury, Venus, Earth, and Mars, as well as asteroids. These planets are also known as the *terrestrial planets* because they have surfaces made of rock. The Outer Solar System includes the planets Jupiter, Saturn, Uranus, Pluto (the *dwarf planet*) and Neptune, as well as comets. Jupiter, Saturn, Uranus, and Neptune are also known as the *gas giants* because they are made of gases. The greater the *mass* of a planet, the larger its *gravitational pull*, so the stronger planets have a stronger gravitational pull than what we experience here on Earth.

In this activity, you will learn about and compare the size of the planets (and dwarf planet Pluto) that comprise our solar system.

Time Needed

45 minutes

What You Need

- grain of rice
- pea
- coffee bean
- blueberry
- cherry
- kiwi

- ✎ nectarine

- ✎ orange

- ✎ cantaloupe

- ✎ pumpkin

  (If the fruits listed above cannot be purchased, plastic fruits can be substituted, or other food items of similar size may be substituted [e.g., gum drops])

- ✎ unlined paper, several sheets

- ✎ newspaper, a few sheets

- ✎ scissors

- ✎ ruler

- ✎ meterstick

- ✎ colored pencils

- ✎ transparent tape

Safety Precautions

Please review and follow the safety guidelines at the beginning of this volume.

What You Do

1. Using the data table as your guide, arrange the fruits, whose sizes are proportional but not to scale of the planets, in order from closest to the Sun to farthest from the Sun.

2. Observe and note the differences in size.

3. Using the meterstick, cut out from the newspaper an approximate circle that is the scaled diameter (see the data table) of the Sun (Figure 1). If necessary, tape sheets of newspaper together to create a large enough area.

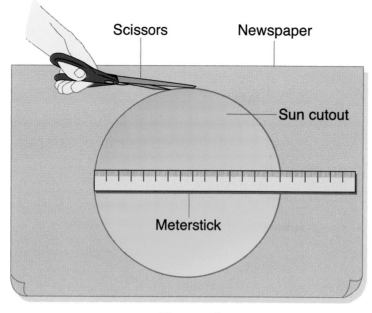

Figure 1

4. Cut out circles for the other planets per the scaled diameters from the data table.

5. With the colored pencils, color the planets.

6. Lay the Sun on the floor.

7. Arrange the planets on the floor in order from the Sun (Figure 2).

8. Observe and note the size differences.

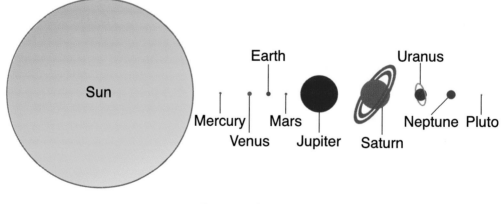

Figure 2

Data Table		
Object (Planets are arranged from closest to the Sun to farthest from the Sun.)	**Scaled diameter (reduced by a factor of 1 billion)**	**Food (not to scale)**
Sun	1,392 mm	pumpkin
Mercury	4.9 mm	coffee bean
Venus	12.1 mm	blueberry
Earth	12.7 mm	cherry
Mars	6.7 mm	pea
Jupiter	142.8 mm	cantaloupe
Saturn	120.6 mm	orange
Uranus	51.3 mm	kiwi
Pluto	2.3 mm	nectarine
Neptune	49.1 mm	rice

 Observations

1. Were you surprised to see the differences in size between planets? Why or why not?
2. How does the size or mass of a planet affect gravity?
3. Why is our distance from the Sun so important?

Our Findings

Please refer to the Our Findings appendix at the back of this volume.

Further Reading

Aguilar, David. *Planets, Stars, and Galaxies: A Visual Encyclopedia of Our Universe*. Des Moines, IA: National Geographic Children's Books, 2007. Beautiful color pictures enhance this children's dictionary of space.

"Solar System." *National Geographic*, 2010. Available online. URL:http://science.nationalgeographic.com/science/space/solar-system. Accessed April 24, 2010. Interactive Web site about the Solar System and the bodies found within it.

———. *KidsAstronomy.com*, 2009. Available online. URL: http://www.kidsastronomy.com/solar_system.htm. Accessed April 24, 2010. Child-friendly Web site with interactive information about the planets in the Solar System.

"Solar System Simulator." Jet Propulsion Laboratory, 2010. Available online. URL: http://space.jpl.nasa.gov/. Accessed April 24, 2010. Allows users to see how the Solar System looks from different perspectives in space.

Tyson, Neil. *The Pluto Files: The Rise and Fall of America's Favorite Planet*. New York: W.W. Norton & Company, 2009. Humorous book that provides real scientific information about Pluto, its discovery, and its downgraded status, told by an astrophysicist.

19. MIRAGES—REFLECTIONS AND RE-FRACTIONS AT BOUNDARY LAYERS

Introduction

A *mirage* is an *optical illusion* that occurs when the *reflection* of distant objects becomes *distorted* due to the *refraction* of light at a *boundary*, such as between 2 different layers of air or between air and water. Cold air has a greater *refractive index* than warm air because cold air is *denser*. Mirages are most often seen at sea or in the desert. A common type of mirage is an *inferior mirage*, which occurs when the light passing through atmospheric layers is refracted, causing objects to appear distorted. You may have experienced this on a hot day while looking at the horizon over a road. A less common occurrence is a *superior mirage*, which appears in the air as an upside-down version of an object at sea.

In this experiment, you will create 2 boundary layers that cause both reflection and refraction, simulating a mirage.

Time Needed

30 minutes

What You Need

- large transparent beaker
- tap water, enough to fill the beaker about 3/4 full
- vegetable oil, enough to fill the beaker about 1/4 full
- measuring cup
- desk lamp with a lightbulb

✎   electrical outlet for the desk lamp

✎   pencil and paper

 Safety Precautions

Please review and follow the safety guidelines at the beginning of this volume.

What You Do

1. Fill the beaker about 3/4 full with tap water. This creates 1 boundary layer (water/air).

2. Shine the light from the lamp on the surface of the water (Figure 1).

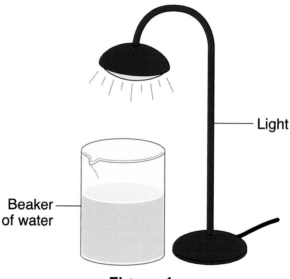

Light

Beaker of water

Figure 1

3. Peer down into the water.

4. Write your observations on paper about the reflection of the light on the surface of the water. For example, does the surface of the water now act like a mirror?

5. Now turn the lamp so that the light shines upward, beneath the beaker with water. That is, hold the beaker of water above the light (Figure 2).

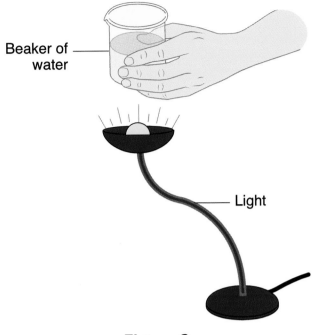

Beaker of water —

— **Light**

Figure 2

6. Note your observations about the reflection of the light.

7. Place the pencil into the beaker of water and allow it to rest at an angle against the side of the beaker (Figure 3).

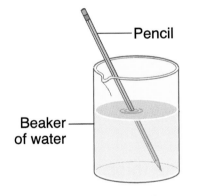

—**Pencil**

Beaker of water —

Figure 3

8. Observe the pencil from different angles, e.g., from above, from below, and from the side.

9. Note your observations about how the pencil looks. Does it look straight or bent from different angles.

10. Remove the pencil.

11. Slowly pour the vegetable oil into the beaker on top of the water until the beaker is almost full but not overflowing (Figure 4). This creates 2 boundary layers (water/oil, oil/air).

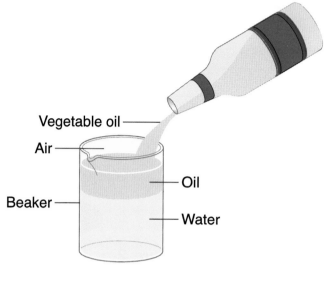

Vegetable oil

Air

Oil

Beaker

Water

Figure 4

12. Repeat steps 2 to 10, especially noting any differences in reflection or refraction where the water and oil meet.

 **Observations**

1. What did you notice when you shined the light on the surface of the water?

2. Did you notice the same thing when you shined the light from the bottom?

3. Did the pencil look any different depending on the angle from which you observed it? What caused the pencil to appear different?

4. What differences did you notice after adding the oil?

5. How did this experiment simulate mirages?

Our Findings

Please refer to the Our Findings appendix at the back of this volume.

Further Reading

Ade, Chris, Jane Wetheim, and Corinne Stockley. *The Usborne Illustrated Dictionary of Physics*. Tulsa, OK: Usborne Books, 2002. Clear definitions and illustrations highlight this dictionary of physics terms, including those related to light.

Cain, Jeanette. "Mirages." Lightscience.com, 2010. Available online. URL: http://www.light-science.com/desertmirage.html. Accessed April 19, 2010. Explains mirages in very simple terms for children.

"Mirage." *The Columbia Encyclopedia*, 6th ed. 2008. Available online. URL: http://www.encyclopedia.com/doc/1E1-mirage.html. Accessed April 19, 2010. Encyclopedia entry about mirages and the different types of mirages that occur in nature.

Stille, Darlene. *Manipulating Light: Reflection, Refraction, and Absorption*. Mankato, MN: Compass Point Books, 2005. Science book for grades 5 to 8 that specifically addresses light reflection and refraction.

"What Is a Mirage?" Physics.org, 2010. Available online. URL: http://www.physics.org/article-questions.asp?id=45. Accessed April 19, 2010. Provides a diagram explaining how mirages occur and offers suggestions on where you might see them.

20. THE MOON

Introduction

The Moon revolves around the Earth. As it does, it appears to change in shape. These apparent changes are known as the *phases* of the Moon. The lunar cycle starts with a new Moon, where the Moon is barely visible. As the Moon *waxes*, or gets larger, we see it as a crescent shape. Eventually, we see half of the Moon in its first quarter. As more of the Moon becomes visible, it is known as the *waxing gibbous* phase. Finally, the Moon is completely visible as a full circle. After the full Moon, its appearance starts to *wane*, or grow smaller, forming a *waning gibbous* phase. Then comes the third quarter, which appears as the missing half to the first quarter. The Moon continues to wane and become a crescent once again until it returns to the new Moon phase. The Moon appears to go through these phases because one side of the Moon is lit by the Sun while the other is not. At the same time, the Moon is revolving around the Earth, so we sometimes see the completely lit half, the completely dark half, or parts of both, creating the illusion that the Moon is appearing and disappearing.

In this activity, you will create an edible model of the phases of the Moon.

Time Needed

30 minutes

What You Need

✎ at least 3 Oreo® cookies

paper plate

✎ white cake frosting in a tube

✎ pen or pencil

Safety Precautions

Please review and follow the safety guidelines at the beginning of this volume.

What You Do

1. Open one Oreo® cookie, separating the 2 pieces from each other.

2. Scrape off the filling from both sides (you can eat the frosting and one side of the cookie).

3. Using the frosting in the tube as "glue," attach the remaining side of the cookie to the top of the paper plate (Figure 1).

Cookie
("new Moon")

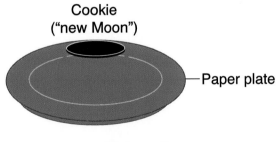

Paper plate

Figure 1

4. Label the cookie you just attached to the plate as "new Moon."

5. Repeat steps 1 and 2 with another cookie, making sure that you get all of the filling onto 1 side when you separate the cookie.

6. Using the frosting, attach the cookie with filling to the bottom of the paper plate (Figure 2).

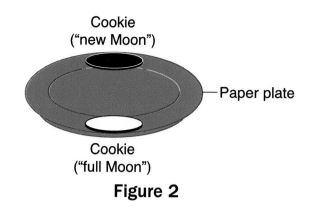

Cookie
("new Moon")

Paper plate

Cookie
("full Moon")

Figure 2

7. Label the cookie "full Moon."

8. Repeat steps 1 and 2, making sure that half the filling ends up on each side of the 2 cookies (Figure 3).

Filling   Filling

Figure 3

9. Using the frosting, attach the cookies to the 2 sides of the paper plate as shown in Figure 4.

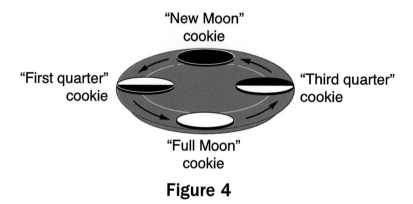

"New Moon"
cookie

"First quarter"
cookie

"Third quarter"
cookie

"Full Moon"
cookie

Figure 4

10. Label the cookie on the left side of the plate "First quarter" and the one on the right side "Third quarter." Add in the arrows as shown in Figure 4.

 **Observations**

1. Which phases of the Moon were included in this model?
2. What other phases could you include in this activity? Using a few extra cookies, try creating models of these phases.
3. Why does the Moon appear to wax and wane?

Our Findings

Please refer to the Our Findings appendix at the back of this volume.

Further Reading

Light, Michael. *Full Moon*. New York: Knopf, 2002. Includes 129 photographs of the Moon taken by the Apollo missions, including photos previously unreleased.

"Lunar Features." 2010. *Merriam-Webster Visual Dictionary*. Available online. URL: http://visual.merriam-webster.com/astronomy/celestial-bodies/moon/lunar-features.php. Accessed July 8, 2010. Images of the Moon labeled with lunar features, including definitions of the various characteristics.

"Moon." 2010. NASA. Available online. URL: http://www.nasa.gov/worldbook/moon_worldbook.html. Accessed July 8, 2010. Official NASA Web site that discusses the Moon in great detail, along with information about the Moon's phases and surface features.

Moonconnection.com. 2010. Available online. URL: http://www.moonconnection.com/. Accessed July 8, 2010. Has up-to-date links for viewing the current phase of the Moon, determining your weight on the Moon, and other fun links.

Simon, Seymour. *The Moon*. New York: Simon & Schuster, 2003. Children's book about the Moon, with many photographs of the lunar surface, courtesy of NASA.

Scope and Sequence Chart

This chart is aligned with the National Science Content Standards. Each state may have its own specific content standards, so please refer to your local and state content standards for additional information. As always, adult supervision is recommended (or required in some instances), and discretion should be used in selecting experiments appropriate for each age group or individual children.

Standard	Experiments
Unifying Concepts and Processes	All
Science as Inquiry	All
Physical Science	
Properties of objects and materials	9, 11, 13, 14, 15, 16, 17
Properties and changes of properties in matter	11
Position and motion of objects	2
Motions and forces	
Light, heat, electricity, and magnetism	6, 9, 19
Transfer of energy	1, 2, 3, 4, 5, 9
Life Science	
Structure and function in living systems	
Life cycles of organisms	
Reproduction and heredity	
Regulation and behavior	

Organisms and environments	6, 8
Populations and ecosystems	
Diversity and adaptations of organisms	
Earth Science	
Properties of Earth materials	11, 12, 15, 16, 17
Structure of the Earth system	12
Objects in the sky	18, 20
Changes in Earth and sky	1, 2, 3, 4, 5, 6, 8, 11, 12, 20
Earth's history	7, 11, 12, 15, 16
Earth in the solar system	18, 20
Science and Technology	2, 5, 6, 8, 10, 13, 14, 20
Science in Personal and Social Perspectives	
Personal health	
Characteristics and changes in populations	
Types of resources	17
Changes in environments	6, 10, 12, 17
Science and technology in local challenges	2, 10, 17
Populations, resources, and environments	6, 17
Natural hazards	1, 2, 3, 4, 5, 12
Risks and benefits	6, 8, 10, 17
Science and technology in society	2, 6, 8, 10, 17
History and Nature of Science	All

Grade Level

Title of Experiment	Grade Level
1. Tornadoes	5–8
2. Recording Earthquakes	5–8
3. Hurricanes	5–8
4. Tsunamis	5–8
5. Volcanoes	5–8
6. Global Warming	5–8
7. Geologic Time Scale	5–8
8. Greenhouse Gases	5–8
9. Creating Lightning	5–8
10. Smog	5–8
11. Weathering	5–8
12. Plate Boundaries	5–8
13. Building a Hele-Shaw Cell	5–8
14. Using a Hele-Shaw Cell	5–8
15. The Rock Cycle	5–8
16. Porosity of Rocks	5–8
17. Mining	5–8
18. Solar System	5–8
19. Mirages—Reflections and Refractions at Boundary Layers	5–8
20. The Moon	5–8

Setting

The experiments are classified by materials and equipment use as follows:

- Those under SCHOOL LABORATORY involve materials and equipment found only in science laboratories. Those under SCHOOL LABORATORY must be carried out there under the supervision of the teacher or another adult.

- Those under HOME involve household or everyday materials. Some of these can be done at home, but call for supervision.

- The experiments classified under OUTDOORS may be done at the school or at the home, but require access to outdoor areas and call for supervision.

SCHOOL LABORATORY

Any of the activities that can be completed at home can be completed in a school laboratory setting.

HOME

1. Tornadoes
3. Hurricanes
4. Tsunamis
5. Volcanoes
6. Global Warming
7. Geologic Time Scale
9. Creating Lightning
10. Smog
11. Weathering
12. Plate Boundaries
13. Building a Hele-Shaw Cell
14. Using a Hele-Shaw Cell

Our Findings

1. TORNADOES

1. The fan simulates the rising, rotating column of air in an actual tornado.

2. The dry ice helps form "clouds" for the storm because tornadoes require warm moist air.

3. A funnel cloud is up in the sky and is in the shape of a funnel. Once the funnel cloud hits the ground, it is called a tornado.

4. When winds at different altitudes blow at different speeds, wind shear occurs and can create a rotating column of air. If that air is sucked into an updraft, the air speed increases, causing a funnel cloud. When the funnel cloud touches down on the ground, it is called a tornado.

2. RECORDING EARTHQUAKES

1. Answers will vary but should be yes.

2. The markings of the pen on the paper are the evidence of movement.

3. A seismograph records the movement of the instrument when shaken during an earthquake.

4. Answers will vary.

3. HURRICANES

1. Answers will vary but are probably yes, as some years have more intense storms than others.

2. Answers will vary but should be yes, as certain areas of the Atlantic are prone to hurricanes.

3. If a pattern is evident after many years, then scientists will know to expect storms in those areas and at certain times of year. This allows people to prepare in advance for storms, build houses accordingly, and plan for evacuations.

4. TSUNAMIS

1. In the P-wave, the spring compresses, and this compression moves along the length of the spring; in the S-wave, the spring moves back and forth; and in the L-wave, the spring moves violently up and down.

2. In the water, the P-waves moved from front to back in the container along the water; the S-waves moved side to side; and the L-waves caused the water to slosh up and down noticeably.

3. The L-wave clearly can cause a tsunami because, in a large body of ocean, a large earthquake's L-waves would cause large waves that would move toward land. The up-and-down motion would create the large waves.

5. VOLCANOES

1. The red water travels through the gelatin as magma travels through the volcano, forming dikes.

2. Answers will vary but may include that the red water traveled in different directions and did not pool in one area.

3. Answers will vary but should be yes, along with an explanation.

6. GLOBAL WARMING

1. There was an increase in carbon dioxide levels.

2. Answers will vary but may include that the burning of fossil fuels increased carbon dioxide levels.

3. The rise in carbon dioxide levels causes a rise in air temperature.

4. The changes in temperature can cause melting of glaciers, drying up of water habitats, and other changes to climate and habitat.

7. GEOLOGIC TIME SCALE

1. The time of human existence is only a tiny part of the entire time scale.

2. Answers will vary but may include information about extinctions, how long certain organisms were in existence, and how long the Earth has been in existence.

3. Scientists used rock layers, carbon dating, and fossil evidence to create the geologic time scale.

8. GREENHOUSE GASES

1. The answer should be yes. There was a difference, with the higher temperature reading in the bottle labeled "carbon dioxide."

2. The purpose was to ensure that there was less carbon dioxide in one bottle, by releasing the carbonation in advance, and more carbon dioxide in the other bottle.

3. By increasing carbon dioxide levels, you can simulate the additional carbon dioxide levels found in the atmosphere that contribute to the greenhouse effect or global warming.

4. Answers will vary but may include that greenhouse gases cause a rise in temperature, which in turn causes climate change. Climate change may result in extinction of species due to loss of habitat.

9. CREATING LIGHTNING

1. There should be a spark that travels between the fork and the pot.

2. This is the same way that an electrical charge is released during a storm in the form of lightning.

3. The reason for the rubber gloves is that rubber is an insulator and prevents the electrical charge from being carried to your body.

10. SMOG

1. The smoke was sucked into the box.

2. The warm air above the smoke trapped it inside the box.

3. The emissions that cause smog can become trapped in the lower portion of the atmosphere because another layer of warm air over the smog prevents it from moving.

4. It would be unhealthy to remain outdoors on a smoggy day because smog contains pollutants that can cause health issues.

11. WEATHERING

1. The clay that was left out had a small, flattened area on the bottom, while the one from the freezer had cracks developing in it.

2. Answers will vary but should be yes. The differences became more apparent as the cracks worsened in the clay kept in the freezer.

3. Rocks that are subjected to extremes in temperature, such as freezing, will crack, just as the clay in the freezer did.

4. Answers will vary but may include water to simulate rain, heat lamp to simulate high temperatures, and a fan to simulate wind.

12. PLATE BOUNDARIES

1. Answers will vary but should be yes, along with the name of the area.

2. No, there is never a day without an earthquake somewhere in the world because the Earth's plates are constantly moving. Sometimes, though, we just don't feel the earthquakes because they are small ones.

3. Answers will vary, but a line should be drawn through the plotted points.

13. BUILDING A HELE-SHAW CELL

1. There needs to be enough space for the materials being observed to fit into the device.

2. The space must be small enough to flatten out the material so that it can be observed in two dimensions.

3. Answers will vary but may include viscous liquids, combinations of liquids that do not mix, soil particles, sand particles, and small crystals.

14. USING A HELE-SHAW CELL

1. Answers may vary but should be no. The materials did not have the same angle of repose because the size and shape of the particles were different and so behave differently when they settle.

2. By checking the angle 3 times, we could find the average angle and ensure that our measurements were correct.

3. Answers may vary but should be that the angle would be somewhere in between what it was when each was poured separately.

4. A Hele-Shaw cell helps us visualize something that occurs in rocks that would be difficult to observe. It also allows us to see a "snapshot" of it in a 2-dimensional form when it actually occurs in 3 dimensions.

15. THE ROCK CYCLE

1. Answers will vary but may include that sedimentary rocks have layers, metamorphic rocks tend to have flakes or banding, and igneous rocks usually look glassy or have crystals.

2. An igneous rock may have been subjected to pressure, erosion, or other processes, causing it to end up in a sedimentary rock at some point.

3. It is called the rock cycle because rocks are continuously made, broken down, subjected to heat and pressure, and change. Though these processes may take a long time, rocks are actually "recycled" naturally.

16. POROSITY OF ROCKS

1. Answers will vary but should be the gravel.

2. Answers will vary but should be the silt.

3. Answers will vary but should be yes. Sandstone should be porous because the materials that make it up are porous, so there is room for water.

4. If there is a lot of empty space in a rock, it will be lighter. If a rock had little air space, it would probably be heavier.

17. MINING

1. Answers will vary but most likely should be that the process was difficult.

2. It is sometimes a difficult process to separate the precious item from the ore, just as it is to remove the chocolate chip from the cookie.

3. Answers will vary but a possible answer is that most mining destroys the surrounding environment. You have to dig up the surrounding area to get to the item you are trying to mine.

18. SOLAR SYSTEM

1. Answers will vary.

2. Planets with a larger mass will have a stronger gravitational pull.

3. Because of our distance from the Sun, life can exist because it is neither too cold nor too hot on our planet Earth. This allows also for the existence of liquid water.

19. MIRAGES—REFLECTIONS AND REFRACTIONS AT BOUNDARY LAYERS

1. There was a reflection of the light in the water.

2. Yes, there was a reflection of the light.

3. Yes, refraction caused the pencil to look different.

4. The appearance of the pencil was different in the water than in the oil.

5. This simulation required the creation of different boundaries, which are among the conditions for the existence of a mirage.

20. THE MOON

1. New moon, full moon, first quarter, and third quarter.

2. Waxing crescent, waxing gibbous, waning gibbous, and waning crescent.

3. The Moon appears to wax and wane because one side of the Moon is lit by the Sun and the other is not, while at the same time the Moon is revolving around the Earth.

Tips for Teachers

General

- Always review all safety guidelines before attempting any experiment.
- Enforce all safety guidelines
- Try the experiment on your own first to be better prepared for possible questions that may arise.
- You may try demonstrating each step of the experiment as you explain it to the students.
- Check for correlation to standards in order to best match the experiment to the curriculum.
- Provide adult assistance and supervision. Do not leave students unsupervised.
- Make sure students feel comfortable asking for help when needed.

Equipment and Supplies

- Most glassware can be purchased from scientific supply companies like Carolina Science Supply Company. Many companies have both print and online catalogs.
- Chemicals and special materials can also be purchased from these companies.
- Many of the supplies and substances used in the experiments are household items that can be found at home or purchased at a local market.
- For some of the hard-to-find items (e.g., extra-large jars), try asking local restaurants, or check warehouse-type stores that carry industrial-size items. For some substances (e.g., lamp oil), you should check with hardware or home-improvement stores.

Special-Needs Students

- Please make sure to follow the individualized education plans (IEPs) and 504 accommodation plans for any special-needs students who have them.
- Provide a handout for students who require visual aids.
- Create a graphic representation of the experiment for students who use picture cards to communicate.

(continued)

- For visually disabled students, provide copies with enlarged print.
- Involve students with dexterity issues by providing opportunities to participate in ways that match their abilities—e.g., be the timekeeper or the instruction reader.
- Read aloud directions for students who require verbal cues.
- Record the instructions for playback.
- Repeat instructions more than once.
- Demonstrate the experiment so that students can see how it should be done correctly.
- Check frequently for comprehension.
- Ask students to repeat the information so that you can ensure accuracy.
- Break down directions into simple steps.
- Have students work with a lab partner or in a lab group.
- Provide adult assistance when necessary.
- Make sure that students with auditory disabilities know visual cues in case of danger or emergency.
- Simplify the experiment for students with developmental disabilities.
- Incorporate assistive technology for students who require it; e.g., use of Alphasmart® keyboards for recording observations and for dictation software.
- Provide preferred seating (e.g., front row) for students with disabilities to ensure they are able to see and hear demonstrations.
- Provide an interpreter if available for students with auditory disabilities who require American Sign Language.
- Consult with your school's inclusion specialist, resource teacher, or special education teacher for additional suggestions.
- Arrange furniture so that all students have clear access to information being presented and can move about the room (e.g., wheelchair-accessible aisles of about 48 inches).
- Offer students the option of recording their responses.
- Eliminate background noise when it is distracting.
- Face the class when speaking, and keep your face visible for students who lip-read.
- Repeat new words in various contexts to enhance vocabulary.
- Alter table heights for wheelchair access.

(continued)

- Substitute equipment with larger sizes for easy gripping.

- Ask the student if he or she needs help before offering it.

- Place materials within easy reach of the students.

- Be aware of temperature. Some students may not be able to feel heat or cold and might injure themselves.

- Identify yourself to students with visual impairments. Also speak when you enter or leave the room.

- For visually impaired students, give directions in relation to the student's body. Do not use words like "over here." Also describe verbally what is happening in the experiment.

Glossary

A

accumulate to gather or collect

acid compound usually having a sour taste and capable of neutralizing alkalis and reddening blue litmus paper, containing hydrogen that can be replaced by a metal or an electropositive group to form a salt, or containing an atom that can accept a pair of electrons from a base

agents something that brings about a certain effect

ages unit of geological time, shorter than an epoch, during which the rocks comprising a stage were formed

altitude height of anything above a given planetary reference plane; usually refers to above sea level on Earth

asteroid sometimes referred to as a minor planet, an asteroid is any of the thousands of small bodies, from 480 miles to less than 1 mile in diameter, that revolve around the Sun in orbits

atmosphere gaseous envelope surrounding the Earth

atmospheric resembling or suggestive of the atmosphere

B

boundary something that indicates bounds or limits

C

carbon dioxide colorless, odorless, incombustible gas, CO_2 is present in the atmosphere and formed during respiration

chemical weathering process by which rocks are decomposed, dissolved, or loosened by chemical processes

chronological pertaining to or arranged in the order of time

climate change any long-term significant change in the weather patterns of an area

comet a celestial body moving about the Sun, usually in a highly eccentric orbit, consisting of a central mass surrounded by an envelope of dust and gas that may form a tail that streams away from the Sun

compaction consolidation of sediments resulting from the height of overlying deposits

composed to constitute; a part of

composition	combing of parts or elements to form a whole
constellation	any various groups of stars to which definite names have been given
continental collision	when continental plates hit each other
convergent boundaries	where the giant plates of the Earth's crust are pushed together
cross section	a cutting or piece of something cut off at right angles to an axis
crust	outermost layer of the Earth
cumulonimbus	a cloud, usually dark, indicative of a storm
cyclone	storm that rotates around a center of low atmospheric pressure

D

decompose	to separate or resolve into constituent parts or elements; disintegrate
denser	having relativity high density or volume in which components are compacted closely together
deposition	the act of laying down sediments
depression	area completely or mostly surrounded by higher land, ordinarily having interior drainage and not conforming to the valley of a single stream
dike	an igneous sheet that forms across other rock formations on parts of a volcano
discharge	as in the discharge of a buildup of electricity
dissipating	to scatter in various directions
distorted	not truly or completely representing the facts or reality
divergent boundaries	where plates of the Earth's crust are pulling away from each other
drought	a period of dry weather that is especially long and is injurious to crops
dwarf planet	a celestial body orbiting the Sun that is massive enough to be rounded by its own gravity but not large enough to be considered a planet

E

earthquakes	a series of vibrations induced in the Earth's crust by the abrupt rupture and rebound of rocks in which elastic strain has been slowly accumulating
electricity	dealing with electric charges and currents
emissions	emitting of poisonous fumes
emit	to give forth
environment	the air, water, minerals, organisms, and all other external factors surrounding and affecting a given organism at any time

eon   largest division of geologic time, comprising two or more eras

epochs   any of several divisions of a geologic period during which a geologic series is formed

erosion   the process by which the surface of the Earth is worn away by the action of water, glacier, winds, or waves

extraction   to take out or remove

extrusion   molten rock that has been forced out

F

fault   break in the continuity of a body of rock or of a vein, with dislocation along the plane of the fracture

fissure   a narrow opening produced by cleavage or separation of parts

focus   the point of origin of an earthquake

fossil fuels   any combustible organic material like oil, coal, or natural gas derived from the remains of former life

fossils   any remains, impression, or trace of a living thing of a former geologic age

Fujita scale   a classification system for the severity of a tornado based on the damage done; also called F-scale

funnel cloud   rapidly rotating funnel-shaped cloud extending downward from the base of a cumulonimbus cloud; if it touches the surface of the Earth called a tornado or waterspout

G

geologic time scale   a system of chronologic measurement relating stratigraphy to time

geologist   a person who specializes in geologic research and study

geology   science that deals with the dynamics and physical history of the Earth, the rocks of which it is composed, and the physical, chemical, and biological changes that the Earth has undergone or is undergoing

glaciers   extended mass of ice formed from snow accumulating over the years and moving very slowly, either descending from high mountains or moving outward from centers of accumulation

global warming   an increase in the Earth's average atmospheric temperature that causes corresponding changes in climate and that may result from the greenhouse effect

gravitational pull   gravitation, or gravity, one of the four fundamental interactions of nature and the means by which objects with mass attract one another

greenhouse effect   warming of the surface and lower atmosphere of a planet that is caused by reradiation of solar radiation into heat

greenhouse gas   any of the gases whose absorption of solar radiation is responsible for the greenhouse effect, including carbon dioxide, methane, ozone, and the fluorocarbons

H

habitat   the place or environment where a plant or animal naturally or normally lives and grows

Hele-Shaw cell   2 flat planes in between which a fluid is injected to model 3-dimensional fluid motion in 2 dimensions

hurricane   tropical, cyclonic storm of the western North Atlantic that is violent and has wind speeds of or in excess of 72 mph

hypocenter   focus of an earthquake

I

igneous rock   rocks formed beneath the Earth's surface or at its surface as lava, formed by the cooling and solidifying of molten materials

inferior mirage   image of an object that appears below the actual object due to the refraction or bending of light waves from the object

L

lava   the molten, fluid rock that issues from a volcano or volcanic vent

lightning   brilliant electric spark discharge in the atmosphere occurring within a thundercloud, between clouds, or between a cloud and the ground

lithification   the process by which unconsolidated materials are converted into coherent solid rock by compaction or cementation

lithosphere   solid portion of the Earth and the crust and upper mantle of the Earth

liquid   molecules that move freely among themselves but do not change in volume

M

magma   molten material beneath or within the Earth's crust

magnitude   greatness of size or amount or strength

mantle   layer of the Earth between the crust and the core, about 2,900 km thick, and consisting mainly of magnesium-iron silicate minerals

manufactured   making of goods or wares by manual labor or by machinery

mass	body of coherent particles and matter that is usually of indefinite shape and often of considerable size
mass extinctions	times at which, during the geologic time scale, numerous species died out at about the same time
matter	the substance of which any physical object consists of or is composed of
mechanical weathering	when rocks are broken down without any chemical change
metamorphic rock	once one form of rock that has changed to another under the influence of heat, pressure, or some other agent without passing through a liquid phase
methane	CH_4; colorless, odorless, flammable gaseous hydrocarbon that is a product of decomposition of organic matter and of the carbonization of coal and is used as a fuel and as a starting material in chemical synthesis
microscope	optical instrument having a magnifying lens or a combination of lenses for inspecting objects too small to be seen by the unaided eye
mid-ocean ridges	any of several seismically active submarine mountain ranges that extend through the Atlantic, Indian, and South Pacific oceans, each hypothesized to be the locus of sea-floor spreading
mining	the industry of extracting, for example, ores and coal from mines
mirage	optical phenomenon usually in the desert or at sea in which an object appears that is not truly there
molten	liquefied by heat in a station of fusion
mythological	imaginary or fictitious, from the word *myth*, a story oftentimes based on a factual event that embodies a cultural or religious event or idea that is often passed down through oral tradition

N

nitrogen oxide	any of several oxides of nitrogen formed by the action of nitric acid on oxidizable materials

O

optical illusion	something that deceives the eyes by producing a false or misleading impression of reality
ore	a metal-bearing mineral or rock, or a native metal, that can be mined
organic compound	compound containing hydrocarbon groups
oxidation	the deposit that forms on the surface of metal as it oxidizes
ozone	a very reactive form of oxygen that is a bluish irritating gas of pungent odor

P

particle	one of the extremely small constituents of matter, like an atom or nucleus
particulate matter	material suspended in the air in the form of minute, solid particles or liquid droplets
photochemical smog	air pollution containing ozone and other reactive chemical compounds formed by the action of sunlight on nitrogen oxides and hydrocarbons
physical weathering	class of processes that breaks down rocks without chemical change
planets	any of the 9 large heavenly bodies revolving around the Sun
plate boundaries	where tectonic plates meet
pollution	introduction of harmful substances or products into the environment
porosity	ratio, expressed as percentage, of the volume of the pores or interstices of a substance
precious metals	gold, silver, or platinum
pressure	force exerted
properties	essential or distinctive attribute or quality of a thing

R

radiation	process of emitting radiant energy through the form of waves or particles
reaction	reciprocal action of chemical agents upon each other; chemical change
reflection	act of reflecting or the state of being reflected
refraction	change of direction of a ray of light, sound, or heat; ability of the eye to refract light that enters it so as to form an image on the retina
refractive index	number indicating the speed of light in a given medium as either the ratio of the speed of light in a vacuum to that in the given medium or the ratio of the speed of light in a specified medium to that in the given medium
regulation	authoritative rule dealing with details or procedure; control
respiratory	pertaining to or serving for respiration; the act of breathing
Richter scale	in which the magnitude of an earthquake is determined from the logarithm of the amplitude of waves recorded by seismographs
rock cycle	process by which rocks are formed, layered, destroyed, and reformed by geological processes

S

Saffir-Simpson scale	hurricane scale used for classification of some Western Hemisphere tropical cyclones that exceed the intensities of tropical storms

sandstone	common sedimentary rock consisting of sand, usually quartz, cemented together by various substances
sediment	mineral or organic matter deposited by water, air, or ice
sedimentary rock	formed through the deposition and solidification of sediment, especially sediment transported by water (rivers, lakes, and oceans), ice (glaciers), and wind
sedimentation	deposition or accumulation of sediment
seismic	pertaining to, of the nature of, or caused by an earthquake or vibration of the earth, whether due to natural or artificial causes
seismograph	instrument for automatically detecting and recording the intensity, direction, and duration of a movement of the ground of an earthquake
sheet intrusion	when sheets of lava cut across rocks
smog	smoke or other atmospheric pollutants combined with fog in an unhealthy or irritating mixture
solar system	the Sun together with all the planets and other bodies that revolve around it
solid	pertaining to the one of the 3 forms of matter; a firm, hard, or compact substance with set volume and shape
star	any of the heavenly bodies, except the Moon, appearing as fixed luminous points in the sky at night
stratigraphy	a branch of geology dealing with the classification, nomenclature, correlation, and interpretation of stratified rocks
subduction zone	process by which collision of the Earth's crustal plates results in one plate's being drawn down or overridden by another
super eon	unit of time from geologic time scale
superior mirage	when an image of an object appears above the actual object due to the refraction or bending of light waves from the object down toward the eye of the observer

T

theorize	to form a theory about
thunderstorm	transient storm of lightning and thunder, usually with rain and gusty winds, sometimes with hail or snow, produced by cumulonimbus clouds
tornado	localized, violently destructive windstorm occurring over land, characterized by a long funnel-shaped cloud extending toward the ground and made visible by condensation and debris
transform	strike-slip fault that offsets a mid-ocean ridge in opposing directions on either side of an axis of seafloor spreading

tropical cyclone   violent storm that originates over a tropical ocean area and can develop into a destructive storm known in the United States as a hurricane, in the western Pacific region known as a typhoon

tropical storm   tropical cyclone of less than hurricane force

tsunami   unusually large sea wave produced by a seaquake or undersea volcanic eruption

typhoon   violent storm or tropical cyclone/hurricane of the western Pacific area and the China seas

U

updraft   movement upward of air or other gas

uranium   lustrous, radioactive metallic element used in atomic and hydrogen bombs and as a fuel in nuclear reactors

V

viscous   having a glutinous nature or consistency such as sticky, thick, or adhesive

volatile   evaporating rapidly; passing off readily in the form of vapor

volcanic eruption   volcano emitting either lava or ash

volcano   vent in the Earth's crust through which lava, steam, and ashes are expelled either continuously or at irregular intervals

W

water vapor   water in a gaseous form especially when below boiling temperature and diffused (as in the atmosphere)

weathering   various mechanical and chemical processes that cause exposed rock to break down due to contact with the Earth's atmospheric conditions

wheezing   to breathe with difficulty and with a whistling sound

wind shear   the rate at which velocity changes from point to point in a given direction

Internet Resources

The Internet is a wealth of information and resources for students, parents, and teachers. However, all sources should be verified for fact, and it is recommended never to rely on any single source for in-depth research. The following list of resources is a sample of what the World Wide Web has to offer. The sites listed were accessible as of December 2010.

American Library Association. Available online. URL: http://www.ala.org/gwstemplate. cfm?section=greatwebsites&template=/cfapps/gws/displaysection.cfm&sec=31. Accessed August 27, 2010. Links to Web sites recommended by the American Library Association are provided, along with recommendations by age level.

Astronomy.com. Available online. URL: http://www.astronomy.com/asy/default.aspx. Accessed August 27, 2010. Web site for widely distributed astronomy magazine; provides up-to-date news in astronomy.

California State University San Bernardino. "Ocean Science Lab." Available online. URL: http://oceans1.csusb.edu/. Accessed December 11, 2010. Contains information and lesson plans related to oceanic science.

Discovery Education. Available online. URL: http://www.discoveryschool.com. Accessed December 5, 2010. Informational site that contains lessons and links for educational purposes.

eHow. Available online. URL: http://www.ehow.com/. Accessed December 11, 2010. Web site that has links to videos on how to do various activities, including science activities.

Energy Quest. Available online. URL: http://www.energyquest.ca.gov/. Accessed December 11, 2010. Web site that has sections for students and educators regarding energy sources and uses; created by the California Energy Commission.

Exploratorium. Available online. URL: http://www.exploratorium.edu/. Accessed December 11, 2010. Web site with numerous science-related activities and experiments, along with lesson plans for teachers.

Geology Central. Available online. URL: http://homepage.smc.edu/robinson_richard/geologycentral.htm. Accessed August 27, 2010. Contains links to several geology Web sites with detailed information related to earth science.

Geology.com. Available online. URL: http://geology.com/. Accessed August 27, 2010. Collection of links to a large variety of geology-related Web sites and a wealth of information related to earth science.

Google Earth. Available online. URL: http://earth.google.com/. Accessed August 27, 2010. Allows the user to view almost anything on Earth, or that can be viewed from Earth, whose images have been captured by satellite photography.

Hawaii Spacegrant Consortium. Available online. URL: http://www.spacegrant.hawaii.edu/. Accessed December 11, 2010. The purpose of this site is to provide educational links and activities to educate students in the fields of science and engineering.

Kidsasatronomy.com. Available online. URL: http://www.kidsastronomy.com/explore_index.htm. Accessed August 27, 2010. Web site for kids about astronomy, space, space missions, planetary objects, and stars.

KidsGeo.com. Available online. URL: http://www.kidsgeo.com/geology-for-kids/. Accessed August 27, 2010. Geology Web site for kids, includes information and activities.

Lunar and Planetary Institute. Available online. URL: http://www.lpi.usra.edu/. Accessed December 11, 2010. Contains information about the Solar System, as well as activities related to the Solar System and Earth/Moon System.

Museum of Unnatural History. Available online. URL: http://www.unmuseum.org/unmain.htm. Accessed December 11, 2010. Provides information about events on Earth that many perceive as mysterious, along with lessons and activities.

My Science Box. Available online. URL: http://www.mysciencebox.org/. Accessed December 11, 2010. Has several hands-on science activities for educators to use in the classroom.

National Center for Atmospheric Research. "Education and Outreach." Available online. URL: http://eo.ucar.edu/. Accessed December 11, 2010. Weather science lessons for educators and information for students is found on this Web site.

NOAA. "NOAA Research." Available online. URL: http://www.oar.noaa.gov/. Accessed December 11, 2010. Web site of the Office of Oceanic and Atmospheric Research; provides informational articles and actual data related to weather.

123 World. Available online. URL: http://www.123world.com/astronomy/. Accessed August 27, 2010. Pre-screened Web sites have links provided on this site. Most are official astronomy Web sites or sites that have consistently provided reliable information.

Rock Hounds. "How Sedimentary Rock Is Formed." Available online. URL: http://www. fi.edu/fellows/fellow1/oct98/create/sediment.htm. Accessed December 11, 2010. This Web site provides detailed information about specific types of rocks.

Science Daily. "Space Exploration." Available online. URL: http://www.sciencedaily. com/news/space_time/space_exploration/. Accessed August 27, 2010. Daily news updates on space missions and astronomy news are provided here.

Science Netlinks. Available online. URL: http://www.sciencenetlinks.com/. Accessed December 11, 2010. Provides links to various science experiments, activities, and explanations.

Scripps Institution of Oceanography. "Earth Like Puzzle." Available online. URL: http:// scripps.ucsd.edu/voyager/earth_puzzle/look_beneath.html. Web site with interactive diagrams of the layers of the Earth along with information explaining them.

SEED. Available online. URL: http://www.seed.slb.com/index.html. Accessed December 11, 2010. Informational site with science activities and links to additional science content.

Solarviews.com. "History of Space Exploration." Available online. URL: http://www. solarviews.com/eng/history.htm. Accessed August 27, 2010. Provides information on numerous space missions related to planetary or solar exploration.

Space.com. "Satellites." Available online. URL: http://www.space.com/satellite/. Accessed August 27, 2010. Explains what a satellite is and then contains links to articles about satellites.

Students' Favorite Geology Web sites. Available online. URL: http://www.palomar.edu/ geology/Students%27%20Favorite%20Web%20Sites.htm. Accessed August 27, 2010. Page with links to geology Web sites selected by students for their usefulness and content.

University of California, Berkeley. "Lawrence Hall of Science." Available online. URL: http://www.lawrencehallofscience.org/. Accessed December 11, 2010. Site designed for educators to inform the public of science programs available, as well as to provide links to lessons.

————. "Plate Tectonics." Available online. URL: http://www.ucmp.berkeley.edu/geology/tectonics.html. Accessed August 27, 2010. Detailed information on the plates that make up the Earth's crust and how they move.

USGS. Available online. URL: http://www.usgs.gov/. Accessed December 11, 2010. Official Web site of the U.S. Geological Survey, with detailed information about weather, ocean conditions, earthquakes, volcanoes, and natural disasters.

Index